When God Was
Effervescent

When God Was
Effervescent

SALEEMAH L. GRAHAM

To order additional copies of this book, contact:
Xlibris LLC
1-888-795-4274
www.Xlibris.com
Orders@Xlibris.com
110929

Dedicated to:

Sanaa and Sade'
Mommy has done enough "living" for all of us. While I know you will have to walk your own roads, I encourage you to always fight for yourself. Do great with your life and do it to the Glory of God.

In memory of:
The late Hubert Andrew Graham, Jr. and Belinda Graham- Terry
Mommy: Thank you for showing me realness and humanity. You pulled no punches and no matter what, you were honest with me. Getting to know the real you help me to see God in His pureness.
Daddy: You were my first "boyfriend". I'm grateful for the time we shared (however short) and I hope you see that your lessons didn't fall on deaf ears. Because of the father I had, I am the woman I am.

Love you . . .

Effervescent—(ef·fer·ves·cent): to come to life; bubbling; vivacious, active, etc. The bubbling of a solution due to the escape of gas. The gas may form by a chemical reaction, as in a fermenting liquid, or by coming out of solution after having been under pressure, as in a carbonated drink.

Cited: British & World English Dictionary 2012
Cited: Houghton Mifflin Harcourt Thesaurus 2010

PREFACE

It was late August 1977, a very humid summer night in the city, and Mona and her youngest aunt, Hope, were on their way to the annual summer carnival downtown. "Damn, girl, slow down! You ain't got to walk so fast; the Silhouettes don't perform 'til ten and I'm tryna light this joint." As they approached the bridge, Hope cupped her hands around her mouth to light the marijuana cigarette, and Mona rested her feet on the third step to fasten her brown and beige sandals. "Ooh shit, girl, look at this!" said Hope, holding in the weed smoke as she nudged Mona. Gazing up from the stairs, she saw the two guys walking toward them. "Which one?" she said to Hope in a puzzled tone. As a Chevy turned the corner, the headlights glazed the area, and she was able to get a better look at the six foot three inch cocoa brown brother wearing brown and beige, but she said nothing. Now Hope was the one speed walking. As they passed the men, a baritone voice bellowed back to them, "Excuse me, miss, can I talk to you for a minute?" "Yes," Hope said sheepishly as she turned around batting her eyes, something she was so famous for doing. Mona froze, her eyes falling to the ground as she was again cast into Hope's shadow. "Not you, the one in the brown and beige," said the brown Zulu God as he walked toward the two young women. He flashed a smile and said to Mona, "I don't mean no disrespect, miss, but I just figured any gal brave enough to wear brown on such a hot ass day got to be cool enough to be on my arm. What's your name, baby?" "Mona," she said as she looked over at Hope who was now giving the gentleman less than pleasant looks. "Well, Mona, I been walking this city for five and a half hours and I ain't seen not one other woman worth me stopping for," he said while his eyes danced boldly across Mona's physique. She knew it was a line and instantly didn't feel so flattered by him or threatened by Hope. Before she could turn away and continue their long walk downtown, he grabbed her by the hand. "I'm sorry, Miss Mona. I should have known that a woman like you wouldn't fall for a line like that. Can I try again?" Mona gave him a long blank stare. "What could you possibly have to say now?" Mona answered. Looking at the ground, he said in a low, shy tone, "Can I please have your telephone number?" She smacked her teeth, obviously annoyed by the encounter, and asked him, "Who should I be expecting a call from?" Hope pushed past the two, noticeably disappointed and proceeds to walk to the corner. "Sheppard, Sheppard Olsten," he said, displaying a wide crooked smile. She pulled a blue ink pen from her beige purse and wrote the number in his hand. Without so much as a glance back at him, she turned away on her brown and beige sandals in a jog and called out to Hope, "Wait up, girl, here I come. Save me a drag!"

CHAPTER 1

It had only been fifteen months since Mona met Sheppard, and already they were married with a child and another on the way. Mona had entered the relationship with a two-and-a-half-year-old little girl named Samira, whom she called "Star," and now she is due any day to have Sheppard's baby. Star's father, Born, was brutally murdered just days before her first birthday and only then did Mona find out he had four other daughters and two other wives. According to his religion, Born was entitled to have as many wives as he could support. Mona found out at his funeral she was wife number two. She made up in her mind that she was finished with love. Then she met Sheppard. He was much different than Born. He was a well-educated navy man without any kids. None, except his verbally adopted son, Rashan, who was his first love's oldest boy. She had gotten pregnant with him after being raped by an older teen at a party, and because of her parents' religion, she was not allowed to have an abortion. So they sent their fifteen year old daughter to Poughkeepsie, New York, to have her son and allowed her to come back home when the child was only nine months old. It was then that Sheppard vowed to always be a father to the youngster. He was only fourteen at the time, but felt it was someone's responsibility to raise the child to be a man. The loser who knocked her up not only denied the child but also denounced even knowing the girl and wouldn't step up to the plate. Why not him? His parents didn't pay much attention to his fatherly antics. Instead they played it off as Sheppard once again being too involved in other people's lives. His mother, Marlo, a Haitian-American woman, thought that her son often felt the need to play savior to his friends and relatives. Once when Sheppard was eleven, he attempted to run away from home to find a distant cousin from Mississippi who had run away from home because she was being abused by her mother's boyfriend. When he was discovered by a family friend at the city's local train station, the man brought him home to his parents with the explanation that he was only trying to get his cousin to see that she didn't need to run away. He deeply felt that he could get a job at his uncle's convenience store and support her until she became of age. It was character traits like this that Marlo absolutely adored in her son. They bumped heads whenever she tried to encourage him to use tact in his decision making. Mona felt very similar about him. Two nights after she'd given him her phone number, he called her to see if he could take her to meet his family. She declined, believing that it was much too soon for the two to get so acquainted. After a three-hour phone conversation, she invited him to watch television with her and her daughter. The rest was history . . . in the making.

Initially, Mah Mah, Mona's mother, fell in love with Sheppard. He was respectful, displayed real home training, and didn't seem uncomfortable with odd questions or glaring stares. In fact, he would often go to her when he needed advice; like the day he asked Mona to marry him. He knocked on Mah Mah's bedroom door, "Hey, Mah Mah, it's Shep." "Come in, honey" she said as he pushed the door open. Sheppard wasted no time and for some reason, Mah Mah knew why he came. "Mah, I love Mona." "I know you do honey, but you sure you kids need to get married?" "I'm sure, ma'am. I've been sure since the day I met her." "Well, you don't need my approval." She smiled and walked toward him with her arms outstretched. Hugging him tightly and placing a firm kiss to his cheek she said, "I would love to have you as my son-in-law." As he left her bedroom like a child leaving for the first day of school, her looks of concern followed him as Mah Mah thought to herself, "I hope my daughter doesn't find a way to mess this up."

Mona was washing dishes in her mother's kitchen. Sheppard walked up behind her, wrapped his arms around her waist and whispered in her ear, "I'm gonna make you my wife." Girlishly, she gave his cheek a playful slap and said, "Boy, get out this kitchen, you see me in here trying to clean." He spun her body to face his and looked her in the eyes as if he was prepared to take an oath. "Mona, I'm serious, girl. I love you and I want you to be my wife." Kneeling down on both knees, he removed the beige satin box from his jacket pocket and opened it. Inside was a gold band with a single diamond in the middle of its frame. Mona's heart fell to the floor! "Sheppard, oh my God, that's a diamond!" "What you gon' say, Mo?" he said, looking up at her like a curious six year old. Before she could display any of her inner confusion or overwhelming doubt, she bellowed out, "Yes, yes, Sheppard, I'll marry you!"

Later that night, Mona went to rehearsal with an up-and-coming singing group called "Impulse." All the members of the group were her family members and they would sing back up for a lot of major artists while they were on tour. Right before Mona met Sheppard, a very popular recording company was interested in signing the group to their label, with the condition that Mona would be the lead singer. They were all very excited about the opportunity and were doing one last rehearsal before their big audition. When Mona entered, the men were chattering about the deal, tour and how life would be once they were "rich." Mona then blurted out, "I'm getting married!" Silence fell over the assembly and the group looked both shocked and disappointed. Then Mona's Uncle William said, "You done went and got pregnant by that joker and threw your dreams away." Mona looked to the ground and said, "I ain't pregnant, I'm in love."

Two months later, Mona and Sheppard decided to tell their families that she was pregnant. They later agreed that it would only raise suspicion about their true love, so they figured they would get married at the beginning of the spring, before she began to show. In April, Star got sick, and they were forced to move into a new apartment due to high lead levels at the one bedroom apartment on Hester Avenue. Once Star was well again, they made plans to go to the city's courthouse to make their nuptials final. That day was August 4, 1978. Upon leaving the courthouse, Mona made a comment to Sheppard that would change the scope of their relationship forever. "I hope now this means you'll get a better job and your mother could finally accept me and my child in her house." Sheppard looked at her like she was foreign to life and without a warning, "Swap!" He slapped her standing atop the courthouse stairs. In the next instant, there was a brief roll of thunder, but it was blazing hot and the sky was full of sun. Mona covered her cheek and looked at Sheppard as if she had seen a ghost. He briskly turned from her and proceeded to walk toward the burgundy 1978 Cadillac Coupe De Ville, calling out to her in a disgusted tone, "Come on, woman. Let's go!"

It was now November 3, 1978, and Mona woke up with pain in her lower back. As she prepared breakfast for her family, she mentioned nothing of her discomfort. Before Sheppard left for work at the cab service, he asked her, "Mo, is this a good day or should I stay close to home?" "Go 'head, Shep, I should be okay. I'll call Mandy if I need you." Mandy was Sheppard's less than pleasant boss. She always seemed to have a problem with Mona calling or showing up at the cab headquarters to see Sheppard. "No, baby! If you go in labor, go upstairs to my uncle's house and he and his wife will take you to the hospital, then they will come get me." "Okay," she said as she handed him a paper bag packed with leftovers from the night before. They kissed and Sheppard left for work.

Later that evening, Star and Mona were watching the seven o'clock news when Sheppard came in from work. "Mo, girl, I got something to tell you, ya'll come in here!" he called out to the two from the kitchen door. "Today, some fool was being chased by the police and he jumped out my cab leaving five hundred dollars and two ounces of weed!" It had been more than a year since Mona smoked marijuana. Sheppard told her after they'd started dating that his ideal woman wouldn't be a weed smoker. Her stopping marijuana made her and her Aunt Hope's hangout fiascos shorter and shorter. They hadn't spoke since the day Sheppard smacked Mona in from of Hope. Hope told her, "You call me when you get rid of that motherfucker." That was about two months ago. "What you gon' do with it, baby?" Mona asked. "Hell, we keepin' the money. Shit, we could pay some bills and maybe go out for a nice dinner before the baby come." Cutting him off, she asked, "What about the weed?" "Oh, I'm a get li'l Rocky and sell it to them while I'm at work. I only gotta pay the little niggers a couple of bags off it." Mona inwardly had other plans, but she knew better than to attempt to share them with her husband. Somehow, Sheppard didn't seem to care that she was nine months pregnant. If she came out her mouth the wrong way, she could without question expect to be physically chastised by him. Before he could exit back out the kitchen door, Mona called after him saying, "Bring me back some fried green tomatoes!"

It was 9:54 PM when Mona heard Sheppard's key turn in the doorknob. Star was sleeping and Mona was folding clothes in the living room. Sheppard came in with a whisper, "Hey, chocolate girl, what you doin'?" "Cleanin' this house," she said as she flopped down on the old sofa. "You been cleanin' this house for the past two weeks and if you ask me you gon' clean everything out of it if you clean anymore." He stood in front of her with a seductive look in his eye and said, "Let me see if I can straighten you up." Sheppard grabbed his pregnant wife's hand and led her romantically to the bedroom. Immediately after their lovemaking, Mona began to feel stronger labor pains. She ignored it and figured she'd go to bed and call the doctor in the morning, but at 2:52 AM, she was awakened by a strong pain around her belly. Gasping for air, she pulled up from the full-sized bed screaming, "Shep, honey, it's time!" Nervous and confused, he scurried about the apartment, collecting Mona and Star's things and getting them both to the Coupe De Ville. After dropping Star off to Mah Mah's house around the corner, the two hurried to the hospital. After out running a police squad car and manipulating his way out of four accidents, Sheppard got Mona to the hospital in a record twelve minutes. "Mrs. Olsten, you are six and a half centimeters dilated. "How long have you been feeling pains?" said Dr. Sandy. "Since about seven o'clock yesterday morning," said Mona. "What!" Sheppard yelled out. "You let me have sex with you and you knew you were in labor? Oh no! Doc, is the baby going to be okay?" he said with a disturbed look on his face. As the doctor laughed, he said, "Sure Mr. Olsten, your baby will be just fine. In fact, you may have helped your wife have an easier delivery. You should be able to meet your baby before the morning's end." With a sigh of relief, Sheppard looked lovingly at his wife and said, "See baby, I guess I'm worth some good." Mona went through nine more hours of labor and pain and at 12:55 PM she gave birth to a beautiful baby girl, Hasheenah Olsten, at 8 pounds 11 ounces. She was nicknamed "Sheenah" by her proud father shortly after her birth.

A little under two years after Sheenah was born, Sheppard and Mona welcomed a third child, a boy named Jihaad. Not to anyone's surprise, Sheppard was not present for his son's birth, being that he and his wife were "separated" at the time. The two would go through spells where they would be on again and off again for months at a time. The last time Sheppard left, he accused his wife of cheating and attested that the child wasn't his. Mona was seven and a half months pregnant then. After Jihaad's birth, Sheppard came back home to his family with a new found religion. He insisted that he be called by his attribute, "Hassan." Mona had her own experience with this religion while married to Born before she had Star, but begun seriously practicing when she was still pregnant with her son. Her attribute was Hadiya, meaning gift. Most people called her by that name now. Even though the two suddenly seemed very interested in following their faith, their relationship still seemed to suffer its frailties. Sheppard would still stay away from home all day only to return home at night, expecting his wife to have a sparkling clean house, food on the table, and ready for sex whenever he so pleased. Mona was lacking her husband's attention, and depression began to draw her back into smoking marijuana; behind Sheppard's back of course. Her habit reignited with her smoking a joint after she had put the children to bed one night, then it gradually became something she did while they were napping or whenever her smoking buddies would come by during the day. Hope, her mother's baby sister, and her two younger cousins, Melissa and Gwen, had soon become a part of the clan. One day, Sheppard came home to find a house full of women blasting music and smoking weed. The kids were all in the bedroom sleeping and the house was a mess. That was the day Mona was rushed to the hospital with two fractured ribs, a broken jaw, and two black eyes. By then, she was smoking weed every day.

Once she was home from the hospital, Mona began to get calls from different women. They would call and say rude things and then hang up. The last time she received a call, a woman told Mona, "Can you pack Hassan's bags because I'm coming to get his stuff." Mona laughed and said, "Oh, yeah bitch, you comin' to get my husband's stuff? And when you do, be prepared to come get this ass whippin' too!" Mona slammed the phone down and commenced to packing Sheppard's clothes enraged. Once finished, she told her twin brother Phillip who was recently home from the service to come sit with the children. She took the bags downstairs and sat and waited for the woman to arrive. After waiting nearly four hours, Sheppard's car pulled up to the front of the building. Before she could leap on him in anger, he threw his hands up in the air and said, "I don't got time for your shit today, Mona." She followed him up the stairs yelling, cussing and crying asking, "Where the bitch at, Shep! You fuckin' her, that's who you been leavin' yo' family for these past couple of months?" Without answering or even so much as looking at Mona, he walked into the living room where the kids were sitting with Uncle Phillip, and picked up his two year old daughter Sheenah. "Where you goin' with my baby?" Mona said, grabbing at Sheppard's arm. Yanking away from her, he said, "My baby's comin' with me!" "What about your son?" Mona screamed to him. "I never thought he was mine anyway," Sheppard said as he walked through the living room threshold into the kitchen. Mona's heart sank and her eyes immediately flooded with tears. Fear and passiveness instantly left. Now she felt she could kill Sheppard! How dare he deny her baby! He knew her to be a righteous woman, who was never promiscuous and only conceived children with her husbands, him and Born. She leaped out at him and before he could fall to the ground, he sacked young Sheenah onto his chest. Mona grabbed one of Sheenah's arms and Sheppard grabbed the other. "No!" yelled Mona. "Let her go, she's comin' with me, I'm her father!" yelled Sheppard. Now the two were pulling the little girl's arms like they were in a game of tug of war. Suddenly, Phillip appeared in the kitchen doorway yelling, "Stop, yall gon' break her arms!" Phillip rushed toward the two and heroically rescued the child from the struggle. Sheppard jumped to his feet and looked down at Mona. "You want your daughter, you can have her! Matter fact, you could have all your kids! You can have all this shit, I'm outta here bitch and I ain't comin' back!" As he exited the front door, Mona sobbed on the floor. She knew he meant his words as she listened to his footsteps down the steps. A very important part of her died instantly. Her twin brother felt her pain, but was too occupied with distracting the children in the living room to offer any consolation. Mona lay out on the kitchen floor and balled for the rest of the night and just like he said, Sheppard never came back. Sheenah was two, Jihaad was ten months, and Star was four and a half.

Sheppard would see his children here and there over the years, dropping by to take them for "rides" where he went to visit women and pick up "something" from some of his male associates. Women would often give him money too, and sometimes he would have to "take them somewhere." He never dropped these women off at houses, always corners or rest stops where they never seemed to "go into" any place. Sheenah thought he was mean for that.

A few months later, Mona had to move to an apartment building on Stormway Boulevard. The apartment was on the fourth floor with no elevator. She would have to do the grocery shopping, laundry, and handle her everyday affairs with all three children. At night when the kids were sleeping, she would cry while smoking her weed. But it just didn't seem to numb her anymore. She smoked alone now, so it wasn't that she couldn't get high enough. Her smoking partners became few after being too frustrated with her being abused by her husband. She was now smoking an average of six joints a day. Her children began to spend more time at Mah Mah's house, since her lights got cut a few months after she moved in. Then her rent was three months late and the building owner padlocked the door. She and her children were now permanent residents at Mah Mah's house. To celebrate the homecoming, her Aunt Sweetie, Mah Mah's sister who lived on the first floor threw a barbeque. That night, Mona and a few of her cousins went out to a local bar. It was there that Mona was introduced to cocaine and heroin. Things would never be the same for her or her children.

CHAPTER 2

This is where I start to tell my story. My name is Hasheenah Olsten, but most people call me Sheenah. If you've read the book from the beginning, you've now discovered that the preface and chapter one is about my parents—their meeting, courtship, marriage, and break up. I say break up because they never got divorced. You know how it is; two people get married for all the wrong reasons and inevitably end up splitting without legally sealing the deal. Well, that was my folks. But enough about them, I believe I was beginning my story. I'll start when I was about four years old (since that's as early as I could remember).

I, my sister, and my brother, were living with my mom at Mah Mah's house. Mah Mah is my maternal grandmother. Her given name was Ethel Parrish. She was the fourth born of eleven children and the outcast of her family. She gave birth to four children: Michael, Yolanda, and twins Mona (my momma) and Phillip. When she bore her eldest son, Michael, at fifteen, she was cast out from her family. She took it all in stride! She'd bore another child, a girl, one year later, and ultimately become a single mother of four after a lengthy failed relationship with her twins' father. She worked full time as a nurse and part time as a maid on the weekends. Her children, however, didn't seem to possess her same determination. Her eldest son, Michael, was a repeat offender, finding himself doing sporadic jail bids for crimes such as breaking and entering and assault and battery to name a few. Her eldest daughter, Yolanda, would end up an eighth grade dropout who frequently ran away from home because she found herself in the middle of her parents' frequent spats. Yolanda and Mona's first born children were only three months apart, Yolanda's being the youngest. However, not to many people's surprise, Yolanda married very young and moved out of her mother's house. Mah Mah's baby boy Phillip entered the service post high school graduation and my momma, Mona (who left school in the tenth grade), stayed home with Mah Mah until she married her first husband at seventeen. Following his death, she moved back home on the prelude to her meeting my father, Sheppard. Needless to say, Mah Mah's house was a revolving door for all of us. That began when my dad left us when I was two.

I liked living at Mah Mah's house because she never yelled at me when I got on top of her refrigerator and sang to her pots and pans. I loved to sing. I think I may have gotten it from my momma, since she was the only one of Mah Mah's kids who actually sang professionally. Uncle Phillip could sing too, but he was too bashful to sing for a crowd. My dad had a nice baritone voice too, but I only remember him singing to the radio. I don't remember the day we moved to Mah Mah's house, but I do remember it being very crowded. At the time, my grandmother was housing almost all her kids and all her grand kids. It was my momma and her three kids, Uncle Phillip and his girlfriend Tina, who nobody seemed to like, and Uncle Mike and his girlfriend Brenda, whom everybody called Khadijah. She brought her son down at the end of the summer so he could go to school with us. His name was Craig, and he was two grades higher than my sister Star. Aunt Yolanda, the only child Mah Mah didn't have to take care of, had a son named Ali. She didn't seem troubled by the idea that she had all these people in a three bedroom apartment. She slept in one room. My mom and her kids slept in another room while Uncle Mike and his girlfriend took the room by the front door. Uncle Phillip and Tina slept in the living room on the floor. When Aunt Yolanda came to stay, she turned the dining room into another room. She and Ali slept there. She would come when her husband's beatings became too severe. Then he would be nice and send gifts to try and apologize to her. She would eventually go back to him and he'd beat her and Ali again. With all this company in the house, none of us kids were ever lonely. Star and Ali would fight like cats and dogs in the house but outside, they would war against anyone who would try to pick on them, no matter how big they were. They were famous in the neighborhood for "jumping' people." Boys, girls, teenagers; nobody was exempt. But at Mah Mah's house, they were rivals. When Star and Ali would fight, Jihaad would sometimes side with Starr and I would side with Ali. It was only fair since I spent a lot of my childhood years beating up on my little brother. I would throw him in the garbage, take him in the closet and bite him and kick him in the bed . . . You name it, I did it to Jihaad. He was always very loyal to me no matter how mean I was to him. When he wasn't looking, I appreciated him for it.

I remember Christmas morning. The Christmas of 1982 was a happy memory. We woke up that morning to a big breakfast. Pancakes, sausage, grits biscuits, and of course—eggs. I hated eggs! But the biscuits and jelly would always make me forget I had to eat them. Mah Mah gave me my very first doll baby that Christmas. I remember her saying, "Sheenah, open this box first." The room got very quiet. All eyes were on me and being the shy child that I was, that only made me hover the box away and try to draw attention to someone else. So, looking at my little brother I said, "Jihaad, open yours with me." He burst into a cheerful laughter, saying, "'K, sister, do wit u!" Mah Mah said, "No, no, little girl, you doin' this all by yourself with everybody lookin'. You the star today, baby." Without looking up, I tore into the box. Stopping at the thin plastic layer, I said, "I can't do it." The room erupted in laughter and my grandmother pulled the box to her, cutting the elastic with a pair of scissors. "Here baby," she handed the doll to me. I looked down at that doll, and then I smiled and shouted, "Thanks Mah Mah!" She cradled me in her arms. As I sat down, I looked in my lap at a very realistic looking doll, who was packaged in a box with the title, "Real Baby" on the front. She sure looked real, big brown eyes, real hair and pecan brown plastic skin. That was the first doll I ever really liked and from that day forward, that was the only baby doll I wanted to play with.

Aside from playing cops and robbers with the boys, and hide and seek with my sister and cousins who lived in the building, I would be carrying that doll around. The only problem was for months, she didn't have a name. One day, I was following my Uncle Mike around the house and I asked him to give my doll a name. "Jamillah!" he blurted out as he walked through the kitchen door. "Name the doll Jamillah and leave me alone!" he said, slamming the door behind him. I smiled and said to my doll, "Okay, now your name is Jamillah." I don't think he even remembered giving my doll her name but from that day forward, she was called Jamillah by everybody.

Momma was very deep into her religion when we lived at my grandmother's house and she and a few of my great uncles had a singing group when they were younger. They would have rehearsal and following rehearsal, they would have study sessions. Funny thing is, shortly after we moved in, Mah Mah used to allow Aunt Sweetie to take us to church. Going to church and hearing about Jesus and then sitting in the study sessions and hearing about other things really confused me. So one day, in the mix of a back and forth debate they were having, I blurted out, "Well, who is Jesus?" An instant hush fell over the entire room and when I turned my eyes toward my mother, she was giving me the "get the belt" look. Fear fell all over me and just like rushing water, all my elders rallied around me giving all these different explanations of who Jesus was. I looked about the crowd in confusion. I wasn't sure if I should smile while they were talking, look to the floor and nod, or try and speak—so I just sat there.

"What's all this damn noise in here!" Mah Mah yelled over the crowd of debaters congregated in her kitchen. With her hand stretched out in my direction, she said, "Here baby, come from round these nuts in here." I rushed to my grandmother's hand and she took me to her bedroom.

My mom had started to stay out a lot more around this time. She and Aunt Hope would go to the bar every week. I can remember she would get dressed up in her fish net stockings and heels and brush her sideburns with an old tooth brush to style her hair. She would grab her black clutch bag and hit the town. Sometimes she would be gone for days. When Mah Mah would ask her where she'd been, she would always say, "It was late so I went to the house with Hope." Aunt Hope lived around the corner in the house with her and Mah Mah's parents. As winter turned to spring, my mom would be gone for weeks on end. One Saturday morning, she'd come home from one of her frequent vacations and she and Mah Mah got into an argument. "Mona, these here are your kids and I'm tired of you leavin' em and not so much as callin' to let me know where you at or when you comin' back." My momma got real mad! I had never heard her talk to my grandmother the way she did this day. She was cursing and putting her fingers all in Mah Mah's face. Then Momma snatched her keys off the kitchen table saying, "I don't need to hear this shit, I pay you to stay here every month!" In the mix of the screaming and yelling, Mah Mah tried to stop Momma from going out the kitchen door. They got into a little scuffle. Nobody actually threw a punch, but me and my sister were afraid. My little brother was so scared, he ran to Uncle Phillip and told him Momma and Mah Mah was fighting. Uncle Phillip rushed in the kitchen and pulled the two apart. A little bottle fell out of Momma's jacket pocket. She tried to scoop it up from the floor but it was too late. Mah Mah leaped out at her. "I knew it, I knew it! You messin' with those drugs just like that Hope!" she yelled at my mom. Momma just rushed out the kitchen door, too embarrassed to look in her childrens' direction. Mah Mah cursed and screamed some more until the water running from her eyes caused her breathing to grow shallow. Uncle Phillip just held her close. "It's okay, Mah, don't cry," said Uncle Phillip as Mah Mah wept in his arms. Me and Star were holding hands and Jihaad was hugging Mah Mah's leg. Now Jihaad and Uncle Phillip were asking Mah Mah not to cry.

My Prayer

    I don't know how I feel but I know I should feel scared. The little bottle mommy had is not good, but what does it do? I don't know how I feel, but I know I should feel sad. Mah Mah is crying and Uncle Phillip is just hugging her, but why is he not saying nothing to us. I don't know how I should feel but I know I should feel mad. Before Mah Mah cried she was cursing, and she only curses when she's mad. I don't know how I should feel, but I know I should feel ashamed 'cause when that little bottle hit the floor, mommy's face changed and she didn't even look at us again. She just looked at the floor and then toward the door. And then she was gone.

    Since living at Mah Mah's house, I had to grow more confidence or at least be more vocal. She always found reasons to have me speak or explain something before a company of people. I think she knew that made me uncomfortable and I also think that's exactly why she did it. She would always tell me how beautiful I was. To me, I was just a copper toned, skinny little girl, with chinky eyes, and a raspy voice. The funny thing is, my singing voice sounded nothing like my speaking voice. That often made me ashamed to speak or even sing. Most of the time, people would say how pretty I was once I smiled, which wasn't very often. Now back to the story.

For the next few months, my mother would stay gone longer and come home less. Then school was over and she began to stay home a little more often. She would sit in the house and play with us kids. She would go out and come home the next day at the latest. One afternoon, right before the fourth of July, she came home with a man. My mother introduced him to all of us. "Hey yall, this is Hank, my new friend," she said smiling and wrapping her arm around his waist. Mah Mah walked up behind the man standing in the living room threshold. As she passed him, she looked him up and down with a disgusted look on her face. "Mah Mah, this is Hank," my mother said, now holding the man's hand. "Umhm, you messin' with them drugs too," said Mah Mah, throwing her hand on her hip. "Mah Mah," Momma gasped! "Get that bum outta my fuckin' house!" Mah Mah said, waving her hand and rolling her eyes. Then she started yelling to my mother about her having some nerve to bring some man around her house when she hadn't been taking any time out for her own children. My mom and her friend hurried out the front door. My grandmother followed the two and locked the door. Sliding the chain across the dead bolted lock she screamed, "And don't bring him back here, I don't trust his sneaky ass!"

Mah Mah's disapproval of Hank didn't stop Momma from seeing him. Hank would come to see my mother every day around the time Mah Mah would go out to work. Momma did listen to Mah Mah's instructions though, she never let Hank in the house. The two of them would sit on the front steps in the building near the front door. They wouldn't do much but hug and talk and give each other occasional kisses. Me and Jihaad would spend our time spying on them, opening the door to steal a peek when we thought they weren't paying attention. Hank was always nice to us. When Momma would yell at us to go sit our asses down and get out the doorway, he would take up for us by giving my brother hi fives and teaching me how to wink my eye and sometimes he'd even give us orange slice candies. That July 4, Momma and Hank took us and all the neighborhood kids to the local stadium to watch the fireworks. Hank let me ride his shoulders all the way home. Me and Jihaad liked him, but Star kept her distance from him. Whenever Hank would give us candy, Star would never take any. Even when he would bring his son Latif around, Starr wouldn't play with him. I don't think she liked him and whenever I or Jihaad said anything about him, she just kept silent.

The good thing about my mother dating Hank was that in the beginning, she spent a lot of her days at home. Majority of the time she was asleep, but she was still home. We liked that because it meant she was more likely to come home at night or the next day. That summer was almost perfect until I met Delores. Delores was Ms. Timms' knee baby. Ms. Timms was our new neighbor who moved downstairs from us after Uncle Gipp and Aunt Jacey moved out with their six children. Uncle Gipp was Mah Mah's youngest brother, only two years older than Aunt Hope and

Aunt Jacey was his wife. She was a pretty fair skinned lady with fine curly hair and Hawaiian features. I remember a day when Uncle Gipp had come home from a religious study group. He was screaming at Aunt Jacey about rumors he heard of her being outside after dark. I could barely hear her trying to defend that the only reason she'd been out was to go to the corner store across the street to get milk for the baby. As the argument intensified, Aunt Jacey opened to the front door and started explaining that Aunt Yolanda had walked with her. As she started to call for Aunt Yolanda up the staircase, she picked up her five-year-old daughter to stop her from crying. After moments of Aunt Jacey's calls to Aunt Yolanda, Uncle Gipp started to scream louder now and before I could make my way to the top landing to look down, they were standing at the top of the bottom landing. My uncle slapped his wife down the flight of stairs while she was holding their daughter. Both mother and child screamed in agony and fear! My cousin was rushed to the hospital with a broken arm.

Mah Mah didn't really communicate with Ms. Timms because they were the only family in the building that wasn't actually related to us. Ms. Timms went to church all the time, but she never made Delores go with her. Things were a little different now because Mah Mah was spending a lot more time at the hospital, working with a hospice patient named Mrs. Guillano. One afternoon, Delores came upstairs and knocked on our door. Star opened it and she asked, "Is your mother home?" Without closing the door back, Starr yelled out, "Momma!" We all stood there looking at her. She was a medium sized girl. Her hair was dark and she had it combed in a tam style. She smiled a lot and her face was really flat. She seemed very friendly, but we all still wondered what she wanted from Momma. My mother came to the door and Delores asked her, "Can one of your kids go to the store for me? I'm cookin' for my momma and I don't want to leave the house with the stove on. I'll pay them if they go." Before Delores could get another word out, Momma said, "Yeah, I'll send my girls. The store is right across the street and my aunt is outside. You gon' pay 'em, right?" "No problem." Delores answered. "They'll be at your door in ten minutes," Momma said as she shut the door and turned to us. "Star, Sheenah, get ready."

I and my sister went to Delores' kitchen door and she handed us a twenty dollar bill to get a bag of sugar, milk, and two sticks of margarine. On our way back to the girl's house, Starr said, "I ain't goin back to that lady house, she look scary." I was nervous, but I went anyway, all by myself. When I got to the door, she opened it before I could knock. "I thought I heard something, thank you sweetie," she said to me, pulling the bag from my hand. She looked back at me and I just opened my hand. "Your change," I said, looking at the floor. "Keep it, sweetie, and thank you for going to the store for me okay," Delores said as she shut her backdoor. Taking off up the stairs with a wide grin I thought, "I can't wait to go to the store for her again." As I walked in the kitchen door with my thirteen dollars and change, my momma yelled out, "Sheenah, come here!" She met me in the living room threshold saying, "Where the money at?" Looking up at her smiling, I opened my hand. She snatched the thirteen dollars and said, "Thank you." "Momma, that's my money!" I yelled. "No, it's my money! You my child and she asked me if you could go to the store. You went so I'll buy you something, but you ain't walking around with all this money. I'ma save it for you, okay." With a confused look, I said, "Okay," and walked to the bedroom sulking. Later, Momma bought all of us some ice cream, but I never saw that money again.

Around this time, my father started to come around more regularly. Over the next year or so, I would see him at least once per month on average. Most of the visit time would be spent with him showering me with compliments and treats, teaching me and my brother about driving and harassing my mother either upon his arrival or departure. I remember one evening on our way back to the building, Daddy was driving fast down the freeway with blasting music. His cars were always nice, so me and Jihaad would fight over the front seat or who would get to hand their hand out the window to catch the wind. This night, I was in the backseat when I heard "Sucker M.C.'s" by Run DMC. I instantly fell in love with rap! Once Daddy got us back to the building, I got out the backseat and he picked me up. Looking me straight in the eye he said, "You're so much like your mother. You feel music. You need to be a singer, baby." I didn't think much about that statement after he said it. I just went on as if he was paying my mother a compliment.

I was going to the store for Delores on a regular basis now and she was always giving very generous payments. One day, she called me to go to the store for her while I was outside playing freeze tag with the neighborhood kids. I ran up the front steps and she gave me the money and her list. I returned through the back way, but something was different. Her kitchen door was wide open. I called her name before I proceeded in to place the bag on the kitchen table. Delores appeared in the kitchen threshold saying, "Put the bag there and bring the change in here." I followed her into her living room and discovered she was home alone yet again. She told me to sit down and she would be back with more money for me. When she came back she sat down on the couch next to me and started asking me a lot of questions. When I tried to get up to leave, she asked me for a hug. Reluctant and nervous, I gave her a hug. Delores began to touch me in ways I knew another person shouldn't touch a child. I felt ashamed immediately after she gave me the hug but her actions that followed made me feel like I wanted to die. She put her hands on me in ways that made me feel wicked and shameful. It seemed as if this went on for hours. Then suddenly, the phone rang. She jumped up obviously startled and I darted out of her living room and sprang out the kitchen door. I ran as fast as I could up the stairs to our house. I ran straight to the bedroom and got under the bed. After being under there, shaking and crying, I went to the living room to find my mother sleeping and the rest of the house vacated. I just stood in the living room staring down at my mother's rested body on the sofa. That day, I didn't blame her and I didn't tell her either.

My Prayer

> *God, something happened to me. And I'm so scared. I don't know what to do, God. I don't know. I only know I need to talk to you, 'cause I feel that in my heart. I don't know if you really hear me now. 'Cause I did something wrong, but I didn't mean it, God. Please help me. I don't like this feeling. I don't like this day. But I know I need to tell you this, right now. So I'm telling you. I'm scared, please help me. I don't know what to do . . .*

It was a while before I would go to the store for Delores after that. Maybe it was because Momma was staying away more often now and Mah Mah never made us go to the store for her. Then one day, right before the New Year came in, she needed one of us to go to the store again. Star refused and at this point, Momma couldn't get Starr to obey her at all and since Jihaad was still too young to go to the store alone, that left me. "Momma, I don't want to go." I cried and pleaded. "You goin'," my mother insisted. After kicking and screaming, my mother beat me with a brown leather belt from Uncle Mike's closet. Then she dragged me to Delores' door to go to the store for her. She abused me that day too. Over the next few months, Momma was home more and I continued to refuse to go to the store for Delores (Momma still kept the money) and she continued to beat me every time I refused. Of course, Delores kept on abusing me.

The day that would affect my life forever was a spring afternoon when Delores sent me to the store for salt, aluminum foil, and a half dozen of eggs. This time when I brought the bag and change, she led me into her bedroom and laid me on her bed. I started to cry, begging her to please let me go home. I even told her she didn't have to pay me for going to the store. She sat on the bed next to me and began to talk to me. She said, "Baby, I don't want you to be scared of me. I won't hurt you. I just want to make you feel good. You'll see, you gon' like it." Then she unbuttoned my pants. I covered my face and cried. During this terrible event, I had this overwhelming feeling of numbness inside. It didn't seem to distract Delores at all. She was putting her hands and mouth on areas of my body that were off limits to even me. I started to feel like I was doing something wrong and I know I hadn't asked for her to do any of the things she was doing to me. I started to feel as if it was hard to catch my breath through the sobbing. I stopped crying and slammed my eyes shut and covered my ears, trying to imagine myself in a different place. My daddy told me once that whenever I didn't like what was going on around me, I could always imagine things being better by using my imagination to go to a "better" place. It always seemed to work before now. While Delores continued to abuse me, I was cringing and wishing I would die before she could finish. Once she did finish, she got up and wiped her face with a wash towel. She looked back at me and said, "See, I knew you would like it." Then she left the room telling me I could go home. I put my clothes back on and walked slowly out her backdoor and up the stair to my house. I walked even slower to the bathroom where I ran hot water into the bathtub. Taking off my clothes, I got in the hot water and scrubbed my body until my skin was red. Mah Mah walked in the front door from work and opened the bathroom door. She looked at me and said, "That's' a good girl honey, you gave yourself a good bath. Now get out that water and let Mah Mah take a shower."

The next morning, Momma woke us up to go to school. I didn't want to go, so I just lay in bed with my eyes open. Momma came in grabbing me up by the arm saying, "Yo ass is goin' to school." I cried out, "I'm sick." She ignored me and sat me down at the kitchen table before a plate of pancakes and sausage with orange juice. I couldn't eat so I just sat there staring at the food. My mother sat on a crate next to my chair and shoved the food into my mouth a bite at a time. I tried to chew, knowing that if I didn't she would beat me. Once I was finished, she snatched me from the chair and led me down the hallway to the bathroom. Once she was finish bathing and clothing me, she sat me back in that chair and I vomited all the food up onto the kitchen floor. Mah Mah rushed in to help her clean me up and she sent me to school anyway.

My Prayer

> *I can't think! I can't think! No, please don't let me think, God! 'Cause when I think, I feel. I feel everything and I hate it! Why did this have to happen to me . . . again . . . worse . . . more! I asked you to help me. Did I do something wrong? I have to be wrong 'cause I feel bad. Really bad and I can't cry it away. I want my breath to stop but I don't want to die 'cause it might hurt. I need You to stop this. Please?*

In school that day, my kindergarten class had to take hearing tests. The teacher lined all the kids up outside the nurse's office and had us sit on the floor and wait to be called. I heard and understood everything that was going on that day, but my mind was completely absent. All I could think about was how I let Delores make me different from other kids. I hated that I still felt throbbing between my legs from what Delores did to me. I hated myself for remembering. This was the first day I would even think about dying. I remember focusing my eyes in on the teacher's aide who was giving instructions to the test, but while she was talking all I could hear was vague background noises. Sad songs jumped in and out of my head and before long, my own thoughts became a major distraction for me. Without even recognizing, I began to bang my head against the wall. The children sitting in line were laughing first and that just made me bang my head harder. Teachers and school staff started to rush over to me and as the guard pulled my five-year-old frame from the floor, I noticed blood running down the wall. The next thing I remember was my momma and dad sitting with me at the hospital.

Saleemah L. Graham

in an oversized crib and my mom was telling me I would have to stay
al for a while. I had been diagnosed with severe lead poisoning and
spent the next year and a half in and out of the hospital. During the course of
this time, I remember coming home from school one day to discover that Delores
and her family had moved out the building. I felt happy, but I didn't know why. I
sat down on the step near her door and wondered where they'd moved to and if
she would find another little girl to do what she did to me. I hoped that that little
girl would be brave enough to tell her to stop. I asked God to make that little girl
strong and help her Momma notice it . . . if she couldn't tell.

CHAPTER 3

I had spent the majority of the year in and out of the hospital because of the lead poisoning and the last two times, my little brother Jihaad was there with me. The hospital set up two large cribs (of which they used to lock us in) in a room with a television and a phone that didn't work. I barely remember having any visits but I do remember what I and Jihaad called "needle time." Whenever the nurses would come to give us shots, we should hold hands through the bars of the cribs and cry. Jihaad would scream so loud that before they gave us the shots, I would tell him to give me his pain by squeezing my hand as tight as he could. He would do it, but it wouldn't work for either of us. Our legs were both swollen and black and blue from the constant shots. No matter what kind of day we both had, I would still sing to him in the hospital until he went to sleep.

Then one day, I woke up and Jihaad was gone. The hospital had discharged him and Mah Mah had come to get him while I was sleeping. I guess she didn't wake me up because she didn't want me to be sad about being in the hospital alone again. The next day I had to take a lot of tests. My momma, dad, and Mah Mah were at the hospital. After the tests, my family had a meeting with the hospital personnel. When the meeting was over, they all came into the room where I was still locked to the crib and tied to the bed. My momma was crying and rubbing my head, my dad was looking out the window, and Mah Mah was smiling at me. When my momma started to talk, she started to cry even harder. Then one of the doctors tried to talk to me and my dad yelled at them and kicked them all out of the room. Mah Mah walked over to me, with a smile still on her face and said, "Baby, the doctors told us some bad news." I got scared. "Am I going to die?" I thought. "But I don't believe 'em," Mah Mah belted out standing tall. I felt better instantly. Looking at my grandmother's pearly wide grin, I started to smile too. "Okay Mah Mah, I don't believe them either" I said, with all my teeth showing. My mother's head sprang up! My dad turned to me with his eyes wide as loft shades. Tension escaped the room so fast that it was like the news had never come to me. Dad took my temperature, Momma fed me applesauce and Mah Mah combed my hair. Two weeks later, I came home. I was six years old.

I found out when I got home that the doctors told my family that I would be classified as a mentally challenged child who would have trouble learning for the rest of my life after all the treatments were complete. I was going to the second grade and school was set to start in a week. I wondered if I would have to go to a new school. Uncle Phillip took us to the park and we played with the Stengel brothers. They'd moved to the block a year ago and they were considered bad kids. It was three of them, Bilaal, Hanif, and Akbar. My sister had a crush on Bilaal. He was a nine-year-old with a chipped front tooth and a foul mouth. His brother, Hanif, was a little over a year older than I and he was on the quiet side, but he smiled all the time. The baby brother, Akbar, was only three-and-a-half years old, but he would walk the street alone like he was sixteen. They would come through the neighborhood with sticks, throwing rocks, and pulling Akbar in a wagon. They had a dog named Magic and everybody was afraid of him. Magic was a stray dog they'd stolen from a rural neighborhood. He would get hit by cars, beat with bats and even shot at, but he would never die. The dog followed Hanif the most. He would feed Magic candy, table food, you name it. Of all three brothers, I played with Hanif the most. It may have been because we were close in age, but he seemed to be the nicest of the three. He would always play nice when it was just me and my brother and he and his brother, but when Bilaal came around he would be mean to me. That would make us fight and before long, Star and Bilaal thought up the idea to make us a couple. I don't think either one of us knew what that meant, but it wasn't long before Hanif would chase me down to play catch a girl kiss a girl. When I caught on to what he wanted to do to me when he caught me, I started to run straight home when he would chase me. I even got bad beating for allegedly dry humping with Hanif that year. Nevertheless, he was still my "little boyfriend" off and on for most of my childhood years.

Me and Mah Mah had gotten to be really close while we were living with her. Momma was never at home, so that meant she would be the person talking to our teachers and making decisions for us. Mah Mah used to cook for us every night when she came home from work and it was then that I would spend time with her. Mah Mah talked a lot. She would tell me stories about her life and why she chose to do a lot of things. She always talked to me in a way that I could understand her, no matter how mature her content was. She would talk to me about everything from being a follower and boys to love for self and somebody else. I will never forget the day we talked about beauty. Mah Mah had taken me with her to the grocery store down the street from the building. While there, she ran into a man she knew from some years back. As they talked, the man kept telling my grandmother how pretty I was. He kept saying things like, "Wow Ethel, she is so pretty. Hey little girl, you sure are a pretty little thing." I couldn't take it anymore! I yelled out to the man, "So what!" My grandmother's eyes got as wide as golf balls. Without hesitation, she cut the conversation short and nearly drag me down the street to the apartment. When we got there, she told me to go to the kitchen and wait for her. I thought for sure I was going to get a beating, but she took a long time to meet me in the kitchen. When she did, she sat down in a chair in the middle of the floor with an inquisitive look on her face and asked me, "Why did you say that to my friend?" I immediately felt calm and answered, "I'm tired of people saying how pretty I am. Pretty is nice but I want to be more than that." Mah Mah's face lit up like a Christmas tree. With both hands, she pulled me up from the kitchen chair and led me to her bedroom mirror. Standing behind me with her palms rested on my shoulders she said, "You said you want to be more than pretty, right. Here's what you do. Stand in this mirror and look for five beautiful things about you that you or nobody else could see with their eyes." Then she left the room. I must've stood in that mirror for hours. I had tried to tell her I didn't understand and I didn't want to look for it anymore and every time I did those things, she threatened to give me a beating. Finally, I stood in that mirror and started talking to myself. "I like that I'm a good person and that I care about people." No sooner than the words escaped my lips, I started smiling. "I got it!" I thought. Minutes later, I had come up with more than a half dozen pretty things about myself. I hurried and gave my answers to my grandmother.

From that day forward, she would keep me under her all the time. She would teach me songs of confidence like, "Anything You Can Do I Can Do Better" and "Greatest Love of All." She would make me sing to her all the time too. She would even teach me about cooking. Hanging out with Mah Mah, I'd learned mostly all of Diana Ross' songs and how to cook spaghetti all by myself.

On my seventh birthday, my momma gave me a birthday party. All my cousins from the building and from my great grandparents' house came. We danced, ate cake, and played outside. I remember my cousin blowing out my candles when the family sang happy birthday to me. My cousin Mosse was there too. He was about six years older than me and I remember him being the tallest kid there. He was one of the first people to come and one of the last kids to leave. Before he left, he wanted all the kids to play hide and seek with him. My momma and my cousins' mothers were all in the back room smoking reefer and before he started counting, I took off running. All the rest of the kids went to hide in the hallways and outside.

"I'm gonna hide in the kitchen." I thought. "Nobody ever looks for you in the kitchen." To my surprise, Mosse found me first. When he found me, I said, "Aww, you cheated, you saw me run in here." When I tried to walk pass him, he pulled me to him and picked me up saying, "No, you caught now." I gasped for air and my whole body started to shake. I didn't look at him. He took me to the side of the refrigerator between the stove and a window and sat me on his lap in a chair and started to grind his body against mine. I felt the lump in his pants, but I just kept looking around the corner of the refrigerator for somebody to come into the kitchen. I didn't want to yell for help because I didn't want my momma to say I was a "fresh tail girl." Mah Mah used to say that only "fresh tail girls" let boys touch them like this. I just let him do it until he finally just let me go. I went outside with the other kids and the game was over. I never played hide and seek with Mosse anymore, but he would always find ways to try and be alone with me. Whenever I would try and keep Jihaad with me, he would bribe him with candy or games or even let him ride his bike. Then he would corner me somewhere and touch me between my legs or backside. It became so normal to me that one day, a distant cousin bought a boy over our house with him and he told me if I let him see my "private," he would give me a quarter. I showed him and in the midst of this, my momma caught me! She really beat me good that day. She kept asking me where I got it from and I didn't answer because I didn't know what to say. I couldn't say Mosse touches me there all the time so what's wrong with showing it. She would think I was a fresh tail girl and I would really be in trouble.

Mosse stopped coming around as much in the colder months. Mah Mah had been dating a white man named Fred for a number of years. She'd been his dying mother's nurse at the hospital and upon her demise, Mah Mah started dating him. He would come by and visit every day and would help Mah Mah buy food for us and take her to bingo. One night, Mah Mah had locked my mother out of the house for staying away for weeks using drugs. My momma had gotten a jack hammer and beat the wooden door in until it was nearly off the hinges. Mah Mah opened the door and Momma leaped out at her. They were hard down fighting for what seemed like an eternity and then Aunt Yolanda burst out the bedroom door and jumped in the fight. She and Momma were rumbling through the house and all the kids stood watching and crying while Fred called the police. Uncle Phillip tried his best to break up both fights, but I come from a family of aggressive women and his efforts were pointless. When the police arrived, they came in and drag my mother out of the apartment like a cheap rag doll. Me and Jihaad raced toward the window to see the cops slamming my mother's inebriated body up against the building we lived in. One of the policeman started choking her while the other lifted her up by the legs causing her to fall to the cement head first. Feeling an instant piercing in my chest, I screamed out, "MOOOMMMYY!!" My little brother sobbed out yelling, "Stoppit, my mommy." Star just looked on the incident with tears falling from her eyes. She showed no emotion. I don't even remember her blinking. Her eyes sat wide open and she almost seemed to be daydreaming. My Uncle Phillip burst into the room and moved all three of us from the window. "Come on, ya'll. Want some candy? Let's go to the kitchen." The next morning, I heard Mah Mah and Aunt Yolanda talking about my momma. My grandmother said she wasn't going to let my mom live at her house anymore. Aunt Yolanda then asked my grandmother about the wedding date. At dinner that night I learned that my grandmother was getting married to Frank and my mother was in jail.

I didn't see my mother for some time after that. I was in the second grade and I was earning all A's. Mah Mah was convinced that the doctors didn't know what they were talking about when they said I would have problems learning and

I didn't either. School was easier now than ever. I felt like I was going to school just to show how smart I was. My teacher, Mrs. Eubanks would tell me things like, "Hasheenah, you are truly brilliant! You can be anything you want 'cause you've got the brains to do it." She was an old white woman with short gray hair and she always wore sweater vests and dress pants—every day. Her glasses were black and thick and people always confused her for being a man. Her voice was very pleasant though, and she made me feel like I was the smartest kid in the world. One day in spring 1986, after coming home from school, I turned down the alley to go into my grandmother's building to find my mother banging on the side door. When she saw me, her eyes lit up like fluorescent lights. She jumped down from the short flight of stairs and lifted me up saying, "My baby!" I hugged her tight and she started to cry. I wasn't sure if Mah Mah wanted me to see her so I motioned for her to put me down and the look in her face changed from being ecstatically happy to surprisingly hurt. I immediately grabbed her hand and smiled saying, "C'mon, Momma, Star and Jihaad upstairs. They gon' be happy to see you too." All three of us sat in my mother's lap, hugging her and rubbing her face while she told us how much she missed and loved us. Then Mah Mah came through the front door from the store. When she saw my mother sitting in her kitchen, her initial look was relief and then disgust. My mother spoke pleasantly to her mother and asked if it was okay to visit with us for a while. Mah Mah replied, "Yeah Mona, see ya kids then find you someplace else to stay for a while. I know you just getting out, but I can't put up with your shit no more. Get yourself together so you can take care of these kids. You can have this place 'cause I'm getting ready to get married and I'm moving outta here." After that visit, I only saw my momma a maximum of three times before Mah Mah's wedding. She'd come the night before and moved her things in to the apartment. After the wedding, we all went back to the apartment and things felt very different. Uncle Phillip and his girlfriend had moved out a week earlier and Aunt Yolanda and Uncle Mike moved shortly after my mom came home from jail. So my momma and the three of us had the place to ourselves now. I had started getting into a lot of fights at school around this time, but none of my teachers would suspend me. I was always sent to sit on the "yellow chairs" and have a conference with the principal at the end of the day. All the fights I had seemed to make me feel calmer and happier. I never really understood it, but I would get extremely mad and at the height of anger get into a fight (majority of times with boys), and instantly, I would be calm after the fight was over. This would be my behavior for majority of my childhood and at times, it would get really dangerous for me. But back to the day my grandmother got married. It was Summer 1986, and I was seven-and-a-half years old. After the wedding, my mom, Hank, and us kids, went back to the apartment. My momma and her boyfriend went into the bedroom and closed the door while I, my sister, and brother sat quietly in the kitchen. Moments later, we heard them start to argue and Hank came storming out toward the living room. "Y'all, come in here." Momma called out to us.

Walking slowly to the bedroom door, my mother laid in the bed looking up toward the ceiling. Without even looking in our direction, she motioned us in and told Star to close the door behind us. She then began to speak saying, "I can't do this. I'm not going to be able to take care of y'all kids. I'm just going to kill myself." Momma grabbed the bottle of pills from the night stand drawer and opening the bottle, she cupped a handful of pills and swallowed them down with a few sips of her canned beer. She scooped another handful of pills and took them the same while her three children cried and begged her with stops, no's, and mommies. Only moments later, my mother sunk into the pillow behind her head and let out a very sullen moan. My brother leaped into her chest screaming and pulling on her clothes, while my sister cried and begged, "Mommy don't leave us." I sat by Momma's bedside holding her hand and looking for a sign whether she would be dying or not. I don't know if my tears were of sadness, fear, or disbelief, but something in me knew my mother wasn't going to die that day. Hank burst in the bedroom door, looked about the room in horror and screamed, "What happened!" Star, shaking and hyperventilating, handed him the empty bottle of pills and left the room sobbing. Hank guided me and Jihaad out behind her and closed the door again. I could hear the commotion of movement and coaching from Hank with light moans following from Momma. Then the ambulance pounded on the door and Star opened it. They whisked Momma off to the hospital. Momma came out of the hospital that same night and when she got back, she and Hank spend a lot of the night and next day running in and out of the bathroom. Hank would sit on the living room couch, nodding off to sleep. It was years before I would know he was under the influence of the drug heroin. However, he would nod so hard and so low that me and Jihaad would stand off and watch to see if he would ever fall and hit the ground. But no, he always woke up right before he was supposed to fall. This was their normal day to us, until school started back. Me and my sister and brother would go to school, dirty, and often hungry because my momma had stayed up half the night doing drugs and running in and out of the building. Star would always wash our faces and get us dressed for school in the mornings while my momma would call out orders to her in a half awake stupor. "Get up for school, kids" and fall back to sleep. "Wash y'all face, kids" and fall back to sleep. "Hold hands and watch them cars" and fall back to sleep. She was always home when we came from school though, even though she was then asleep also. We didn't get much for Christmas that year. Hank and Momma spent all the welfare money getting high and whenever Star complained about it, Momma yelled and talked about holidays being cynical and commercial.

One day after school that winter, we came home from school and Momma met us on the corner. "Hey, Momma, why you outside?" my brother asked. "They locked us out." my mother said with a helpless look in her eyes. "My own family locked me and my kids out in the cold." Me and Star looked at each other then at my mother. Momma then said, "Y'all gon have to go stay with your Aunt Yolanda until I can get a place." Hank and my momma had broken into the bathroom window to get back into the apartment. Me, Jihaad, and Star, sat outside on the stoop and waited. Then Hank came down looking sleepy and sluggish. He turned to us and said, "Y'all alright? I'll be back; I'm going to pick up your aunt. Your mother will be right down." Momma never came back downstairs, but me and my siblings sat on the stoop until the sun began to set.

When Aunt Yolanda came to get us, she was by herself. She got out of Hank's truck and stood on the corner of the dead end street by our building. She acted like coming to get us that night was one big secret. We all walked over to her and she greeted us with tight hugs and forehead kisses saying, "Y'all hungry? Y'all coming to my house to stay with me and Ali." Then my mom finally came downstairs. She and her boyfriend piled five plastic bags of our stuff in the back of the truck and Momma kissed and hugged us, reeking of alcohol. As Hank drove us away, Momma shouted, "I'll be to see y'all tomorrow."

CHAPTER 4

When we got to Aunt Yolanda's house that night, Ali came running to the door to meet us. He was happy and pulling all our bags in as if they were gifts for him. We all said nothing, but instead gave each other looks of sadness and confusion. There was a man sitting on the couch and my aunt walked in waving at him saying, "Oh, that's my boyfriend Tiny. He gon sleep out here with me." Then my aunt walked us into the only bedroom in the apartment and said, "Y'all gon sleep in here with Ali." There was only a twin bed in the room, so Ali and Starr moved the mattress to the floor. Jihaad and Ali slept on the mattress and me and Starr slept on the box spring. The next day, we didn't go to school and my momma didn't come to see us either. In fact, it was months before I saw her again. As those months passed, our sleeping arrangements in Ali's room would go from two and two to three and one. Ali started to complain about having to share his room and bed with us so soon, he went back to sleeping by himself on his mattress and the three of us would sleep on the box spring. Then one day, Tiny came in with a box spring he'd found and that became the "bed" we slept on, while Ali slept on his mattress and box spring alone. Before long, the springs started to poke out and it became even more difficult for the three of us to sleep together. Not to mention the idea we were eight, ten, and six-and-a-half.

One Saturday after the weather broke, I was supposed to be outside playing with the neighborhood kids, I snuck off the block to Mah Mah's old apartment. It was a little less than a mile away, so I didn't mind taking the trip alone. I walked up the back stairs to and looked in the bathroom window to see my mother dumping a packet of white powder onto a broken mirror. I just looked on quietly as my mother and her boyfriend took turns breathing the powder into their noses. My mother paced the bathroom floor with her eyes tearing while her boyfriend sat on the commode with his eyes shut pressed up against the wall. Then she saw me. "Sheenah? Oh, my baby came to find her Momma!" my mother shouted as if she was glad I came looking for her. I smiled in disbelief. I thought for sure that If she knew I saw what she'd just done, she would have beat my behind, but instead, she ran around to the backdoor to let me in. Hank looked ashamed and yet still sleepy.

He walked out the front door as I stood in the bathroom doorway and talked to my mother. I just started spilling all kinds of questions like, "Where you been? When you coming to get us? Where have you been living? Did you find a new place like you said before?" The only answers I got from my mother that day were, "Mommy loves you, Sheenah. You know I want the best for y'all and I'm coming to get y'all soon." My mother hurried me along with a dollar bill and a promise to come and get us from my aunt's house in about two weeks. When I got back to my aunt's neighborhood, no one even noticed that I'd left. I never told my sister and brother about that encounter. I just waited for Momma to hold true to her word. She didn't come and get us in two weeks because in less than two weeks, she was in jail again. My mother spent about six months incarcerated. We visited her about five times of that time. When she came home that fall, she and Aunt Yolanda sat down to talk about when she would be coming to get us for good. "Two months." Momma answered. I'm going down to welfare in the morning to explain my situation and show them my parole papers so I could get the benefits. I will look for a place and when I get it, I'll get my kids." "Okay, I could work with that, Mona—but you got to get your kids." My momma never came to get us. A few weeks later, one of my older cousins came to tell us that my momma was back in jail. My aunt was furious! She cussed and slammed things and said over and over, "Who gon get her kids?" When we went to sleep on that box spring that night, I wondered what if my mother was thinking about us the way I was thinking about her.

Prayer

> *Please give me a sign. I thought things would get better. I don't understand. I though life would be different. My eyes burn from the things I've seen. My ears pain from the things I heard. My heart aches from the hurt I've known. My mind burns with confusion. An illusion of hope is all I'm pleading. I'm desperate and helpless. I'm angry and . . . What else needs to happen for change to come for me?*

A few days later, we were coming home from school and found my aunt standing on her porch at her neighborhood complex building. She met us to tell us she was being "put out" and that we would be going to live with my grandmother's sister, Lattie, who lived in the family building on the second floor. During school hours, Mah Mah had come down from the suburbs to ensure that our move to Aunt Lattie's would be official. That afternoon, Aunt Yolanda packed our five plastic bags and we drag them all the way to the building. It was October 1987.

As we drag the bags through the block amongst our playmates, classmates, and friends, I felt ashamed and embarrassed. The plastic bags busted and we found ourselves losing clothes and having to throw shirts and pants alike over our shoulders. My sister didn't seem to be bothered by it at all. When the kids from the neighborhood would laugh or asked us what we were doing or what was wrong. She smiled and answered all their questions—with confidence. When we got to Aunt Lattie's house, she welcomed us in and had all three of us sit at her kitchen table. Then her three daughters came in, Riana was nine, Ruby was seven, and Reece was only four years old. Aunt Lattie stared to ask us questions. "Do y'all know where ya Momma at? Do you know what ya Momma did? Do you love ya Momma?" and all kinds of questions we didn't really have answers to. Then she started making food. During the first meal at Aunt Lattie's house, I felt like they were watching our every move. She asked Jihaad if he knew how to eat with a fork and had her oldest daughter Riana do a demonstration. Whenever one of us would drop food off our forks, she would make Riana "show us again." At the end of the night, she allowed us time to take a bath—all three of us at the same time. None of us really made a big deal about it, we just did as we were told and went to bed. That night, my sister slept in the room with Riana, I slept with Ruby and Reece, who shared bunks beds and my bother slept in a room that was an addition to Ruby and Reece's. That was the room their elder brother Jeremy would sleep in when he came to visit. Jeremy was about eighteen years old and he was my uncle Carl's; their father's son from a previous marriage. He didn't really come that often, so it sort of felt like Jihaad had a room to himself. That was the sleeping arrangement for about four or five months.

Aunt Lattie was very sick. She had multiple sclerosis and it caused her to be in the hospital very frequently. When she was in the hospital, her husband, Uncle Carl would be the overseer, but my cousin Riana would be in charge. She cooked the food, did the laundry, and gave out chores. She even decided what all the younger children in the house would wear from day to day. My sister Starr was in fact the oldest, but during this period in my life, I don't remember her being too vocal. However, things were changing tremendously for me in that regard.

Riana didn't like me very much. She would be my friend for a few days and then think up a reason for us to have a fight. I could never really beat Riana because she knew karate and would use it on me every time we got into it. Star would always fight her for me though and she would always win. Ruby was weird. She always wanted me to make jokes and play dolls with her, but she never really talked about anything. Reece was a sweetheart. She was the baby of the house and she always tried for people to get along, but if you made her mad, her anger was ferocious. Shortly after moving to Aunt Lattie's house, I remember taking a long nap and when I woke up, the house was empty. I looked around outside and about the neighborhood, but I couldn't find anybody. I spent some time wandering around before I realized Aunt Lattie's car was missing from the driveway. Shortly after my discovery, her 1984 red Monte Carlo turned the corner and all the kids were yelling to me out her windows. "Sheenah, you missed it! We went to Sizzler." my sister said. "We had fun too!" Riana said in a snarling tone. The smaller kids followed Aunt Lattie upstairs. She never even looked at me. As Star was scurrying behind Aunt Lattie and the little kids, I called out to her. "Star, come back and play with me!" She jumped down the short flight of stairs in the alley and said, "What's wrong?" "Why y'all didn't take me out to eat too?" I asked my oldest sister. "I don't know," she said to me as if she was unaware of my maltreatment. Then she breezed past me through the alley and yelled, "C'mon!" as she sprinted through the parking lot to play jump rope with the neighborhood kids. When we came in the house that evening, I tried to wait for Aunt Lattie to get off the phone, but she just seemed to be occupied with something all the way up until bedtime. We ate dinner and then my aunt ordered us to bath time and then to sleep. I never got to ask her why she didn't wake me up to go to the restaurant.

Prayer

Whatever is happening to me right now, I want it to stop! If I gotta live like this, I don't wanna live at all! I'm gonna go off! I can feel it! God, please don't let me go off. Or maybe you can just let me go off . . . this once . . . so I can feel better. And forgive me afterward. Amen.

Aunt Lattie's house was very organized. Everything was done at a certain time. Breakfast was always between seven and eight o'clock in the morning—even in the summer time. Dinner was between five thirty and six and laundry days were split during the week. My cousins washed their clothes on Tuesdays and we washed our clothes on Thursdays. Everybody washed their sheets on Saturday. My cousins washed sheets on Mondays too, because they all wet the bed. Aunt Lattie's family was practicing my mother and father's religion when we first got there so basically, life was very familiar and comfortable early on. Strange enough, a few months after we moved in, Aunt Lattie had gotten really sick and was in the hospital for a while. When she came home the end of that winter, she took us to church. Again, I was confused, but I'd learned from the last time not to ask questions. We had only been going to church about a month and Aunt Lattie put all of us on the choir. About a month after that, I got baptized. It was March 1988.

On my first day of rehearsal, I just moved my lips to the words. I didn't call it lip syncing because my understanding of lip syncing is that you appear to be singing and you're really not. I didn't try to fool the lady on the piano, I just didn't want to sing with the choir because they didn't sound good. Then she singled me out. "Young lady, come to this microphone and sing it all by yourself," she said to me. "I don't know the words." I replied and motioned to take my seat. "No you won't, stand up here now!" she said, standing up from the piano. The rest of the group sat down and that lady made me sing the entire song in front of the choir. I stood in front of the mic very nervous. The old lady started playing the organ and she pointed to me when it was time to sing. Nervously, my eyes darted over the lyrics on a hymnal in front of me. Once I made it through the first verse, I shut my eyes and sang it again, this time louder. It was like I could feel every word through my body. Once the choir joined in on the chorus I mentally left my body and was totally in my heart. I started singing my emotions, fear completely left! When the song ended, my sister and brother clapped and cheered and my cousin Riana rolled her eyes and turned toward the exit. When we got in the car that night, nobody said anything. Then the lady from the piano walked up to my aunt's car window and said, "Will y'all be here Sunday?" I want your little girl to sing a solo." Aunt Lattie glanced through her rear view mirror directly at me and answered, "Yes, we will." Waving to the lady, we drove off and didn't return to the church again for more than two weeks. I don't think I was really surprised about not being able to sing the solo. I think I was more shocked at how my aunt would beat you for lying but lied to the woman about coming back to church that week. Needless to say, I was singing even more after that. I sang whenever I got a chance. Mostly, I would sing around the house, to myself and maybe some friends but never in front of an audience. I just felt that the experience at the church just opened me up to a new way to express a lot of my feelings of sadness, loneliness and even anger.

Prayer

> *God, you gave me a song. And I thank You for a song. I can sing it when I'm happy. I can sing it when my pain is too great. I can sing it when I don't know what to sing. And it feels better every time I sing it. Sometimes, I sing it for hours, sometimes even days. But I sing it, and it all goes away. Only thing is, the melody only lasts as long as I feel it. And when I feel again, I hurt again, and I sing again. And again, the cycle begins.*

I was a little under ten years old and of all the girls in the house, my hair was the longest. Since I couldn't really do my own hair and it began to be a hassle for anyone to style it, Aunt Lattie sat me in her kitchen one day and gave me a perm. She said the perm was for curly hair and that it wouldn't take away my curls, just soften my hair. When she was finished, a lot of my hair had come out in the wash. Star wondered what happened and asked my aunt about the perm. She told my sister, "Shut up, girl! At least now somebody can comb that stuff." I was devastated but Jihaad made me feel better by saying, "You still look like Momma."

Aside from singing, I liked to play the dozens growing up. I would never start trouble, but I would always finish it. All the kids in the house used to really like it too, until they were made the bunt of my jokes. One day on a rainy fall afternoon, me and my cousin Reece were making jokes about each other. She went on about my skinny legs and long feet and I joked about her bedwetting and stuttering. I could tell I was winning the bout because of the laughs I was gaining over her.

Out of nowhere, she got serious and started yelling and crying. Aunt Lattie came out he bedroom yelling to me, "And what about you, Sheenah? You're ugly and dirty and stinky too! Matter of fact, you can get the fuck out my house, now laugh at that!" The whole room got silent and everybody looked at me. I stood in the middle of the hallway, embarrassed and afraid. Moments later, Aunt Lattie stormed down the hallway toward me and shoved me in the chest against the front door. "Get your stinky dirty shit you came here with and get the fuck outta my house!" I looked up from the floor at my sister and brother who were standing in one of the bedroom doorways. "Now!" my aunt yelled, now tossing clothes and toys on top of me. I gathered a few articles of clothes from the floor and as I got up from the floor, she threw my doll Jamillah at me too. Riana hurried back to the door with my book bag. I pulled it from her and couldn't help but notice the smile on her face. Then Aunt Lattie opened the front door and when I walked out, she slammed the door. Being eight and a half, I knew it was wrong to throw a kid out on the street, but my pride wouldn't let me try and knock on the door. I stuffed the remainder of my things into my book bag and walked out the building, holding my doll Jamillah. Walking down the block, I felt all alone. All kinds of questions danced around in my head. "Where am I going to go? Why did she kick me out? Why didn't Star speak up for me? Why didn't she and Jihaad come with me? What did I do so wrong?" The most important question however, was the one I acted on. "Where is my momma?"

I walked in the rain to my great grandparents' house about two miles away from the building. When I got there, all my family members seemed happy to see me. They all said things like, "Hey, Sheenah, girl, come gimme a hug. What you doing here?" My reply was the same to everyone. "I'm looking for my mother, you seen her?" On all three levels of the house, nobody was able to offer me any answers. Coming down the back steps from the second floor, I ran into my cousin Mumin. He was Aunt Hope's fourteen-year-old only child and she was my godmother, so that made him my godbrother. "Sister Sheenah, what's up?" he said to me, carrying a bike up the stairs. "Where's your mom, I need her to help me find my mother." Mumin got instantly excited and said, "I know where she at! I'll take you to her house, she lives around the corner." Mumin put me on the back of his ten speed and whisked me to a building on the corner of Plum Place and sixteenth. "Go around the back and go down those steps on the outside of the building. When you get in, go straight until you can't go no more and make a left." Then he was speeding off and I was standing at the back of a dark building, guessing the direction to go to find the steps my godbrother directed me to. "It's a basement." I thought the further I went down the steps as it continued to get darker and darker. Suddenly I heard the voices of two men coming out of the basement. I froze and clutched my doll to my chest. "Hey little girl, who do you belong to?" asked one of the men with a friendly look on his face. "Mona, I'm her daughter." I said my eyes now peering further down the dark path. "Yeah, I'll get somebody to take you to her—Lay Lay!" Seconds later, a tall skinny woman with gray hair emerged from the darkness with a lighter blazed for light. "Come on baby, Imma take you to ya mommy."

"Who is it?" a man's voice yelled after the lady banged loudly on the iron door. "It's Lay Lay, somebody out here for Mona." the lady yelled back. When the door finally opened, two men and a lady came out and as I looked into the room, Hank was standing on the far side of a bed. A woman was sleeping in it so I let the lady's hand go and walked over to the bed. I looked down at my mother who seemed to be in a deep sleep. Hank yelled her name about five more times and then I took it upon myself to try and wake her. I sat down on the bed next to her and shook her shoulder strongly. "Mommy, it's me." I said calmly. Her eyes opened and when she saw it was me, they opened wider. She sat up on the bed and said, "Sheenah, oh my God, my Sheenah!" My mother hugged me to her heart so tight I could feel the beat. Then I felt a teardrop roll down the side of chin. I looked up at my mother's face shining with tears and said, "Momma don't cry. I'm safe now. I'm here with you." That night I slept in that basement with my mother and Hank. Momma slept in the middle with me spooned against her and Hank slept all the way to the other side of the bed. I slept in the clothes I'd worn over there and my momma gave me one of her sweaters to wear over that to keep warm in the cold basement. The next morning when I woke up, Momma washed my face and before I left out for school, Hank stopped me saying, "Sheenah, wait!" Rushing over to me, he gave me two dollar bills and said, "Make sure you eat something before you get to school. When you get back, I'll give you more money so you can eat again."

When I left the basement, I didn't realize how late it was. My only concern was dodging Division of Youth and Family Services (DYFS), since Aunt Lattie would always threaten to call them to come and get me when I said or did something she didn't like. Once I got to school, all the doors were closed and there were no kids in the yard area. I knew better than to try and get into school without being accompanied by an adult. The school would call DFYS for sure if I'd done that. So instead of roaming the streets, I stopped in the corner store and got me some snacks and headed to my great grandparents' house (where I assumed Momma would be by now, since she hung out there all the time and it was so close to the basement). The clock on the wall in the store said 10:17 AM.

When I got to my great grandparents' house, it was like it was three o'clock in the afternoon. People were walking in and out of the basement there and all three floors were filled with family members. My great grandmother lived on the first floor. She was a church going, very strict woman who loved to cook and play gospel music. She was the mother of her church. I didn't know what that meant at the time, but it made me feel like I needed to be on my best behavior around her and I did! The second floor was where my great grandfather lived. He was sick with cancer and my older cousins and great aunts would care for him when he wasn't in the hospital. A few of them even lived there with their families. On the third floor was where my great aunt/godmother Hope and her son Mumin lived. When I got there, Mumin was in school, but my other boy cousins were all there. They were all my godbrothers too, since Aunt Hope was their godmother. Going there and hanging out all day with them was some of the most fun times of my childhood. Mosse lived there too, but Mumin kept such a close eye on me that I was never left alone over there. When Mumin wasn't around, it was my oldest godbrother Saladin that took care of me. He was short for his age, but very good with his hands. By that, I mean he could fight. His dad, my third cousin from Momma's singing group, put him in boxing school at six years old and he took full advantage of his training. Whenever Mumin would get into fights in the neighborhood, my great uncles would go and get Saladin. Whenever Saladin wasn't available, they would call my Aunt Yolanda's son Ali. At this time, they were living at my great grandparents' house too. Ali wasn't scared of anything! He would always get into fights and win majority of them. Those he didn't necessarily "win" he put up a good fight. Watching him in action was like watching television. I had pretty decent relationships with all seven of the boys in the house to the extent that it was second nature for me to gravitate toward them during my playtimes (even before Aunt Lattie kicked me out). For the next week and a half, when I would miss school, I would hang out at the house with them, listening to rap music, cursing, learning to fix bikes and watching them talk with lots of different girls. The last day I attended school from living with my mom in the basement, I arrived to school early and happened to see my teacher talking to two ladies. One of the ladies had a suitcase with her and instantly I knew she had to be a DYFS worker. As soon as it dawned on me to take a run for it, all three of the women looked in my direction and saw me taking off. My teacher called to the guard to stop me, but he was unsuccessful. I was extremely fast for a fifth grader!

Before I knew it, I was halfway thru the school field and headed up toward the building my aunt lived in. "That's not home, Sheenah" I said to myself. Dashing in the other direction, I headed toward the side of the parkway. I ran and ran until I was so tired that I couldn't swallow. I was shaking all over and scared to go into a store to buy a drink in fear that DYFS would see me and trap me in. Headed back down the hill toward my great grandparents' house, I stopped to rest on the side of an abandoned house. "They can't see me from here" I thought. I sat down on the cement Indian style and put my head down. As soon as I closed my eyes, I could see Jihaad. "What if they gave him to DYFS and the only way they would let him go is if I went with them." I started to cry. Then I started to weep and yell and moan. I cried so hard, I could feel my insides shaking. I felt so helpless, hurt, ashamed, and lonely. Nobody could help me. Not even my mother. Then I got really, really mad. My heart started to race and my face got hot. I need to feel like I was in control of something. I need to feel strong. All the kids were in school, so I couldn't pick a fight and the block I was on was quiet and nearly vacant. I reached in my pocket and pulled out two balled up napkins. "Let me find some matches"

I thought. Walking toward the back of the vacant house, I found a lighter with the back broken off. I set my napkins on fire and threw it on top of an old trashcan. As the fire grew, so did my excitement! I started looking for more things to throw into the flames. I threw newspaper, old clothes, and more garbage in the fire and when it was as big as me, I decided to leave. "Oh no, I can't get past the flames!" I was trapped on the side of the old house with a growing fire. I started hearing voices. "Ooh it's a fire over here, call 911." I could hear a woman telling someone. The gate behind me was tall, but I had no other choice. I shut my eyes at the top and leaped over. That gave me more excitement! Thankfully, I was gone before the police arrived.

Ballad of an Abandoned Child

I woke up in life
Bare and tender
Looking for home
Innocent and naive, eager for life
To be let down and shocked
Caught off guard by pain
Rare but close
Unfamiliar but sure
Peculiar yet definite
Now I'm looking for home
Thru the windows of empty promises and happy lies
Anticipations that have zeal
Yet no effort
I am looking for home
On doorsteps of letdowns and sad goodbyes
Ringing bells that go deaf on the ears of my beloved
Sitting on this stoop
ALONE—Looking for home
Longing for truth, Longing for who?
Mother, father, family, peace
And YOU
Can't give it to me
I can only get it at
Home

I didn't go back to my great grandparents' house until nearly five o'clock. When I got there, Mumin told me the DYFS was there looking for me, but he told them nobody had seen me. He also told me that my mother told them she would call them when I got back. In shock I told him he was lying. Without even answering, he told me to hide out upstairs with him in the attic. I declined and proceeded into the house to find my momma. When I got to the second floor, Star was up there sitting and talking with Ali. As soon as she saw me, she blurted out, "Aunt Lattie said you better come back with me or she gonna let DYFS take you away." What happened to "Hey Sheenah, are you okay? I missed you. Are you hurt?" Still I couldn't be mad at my sister. I got sad all over again. Looking down at the floor, I told Star I wasn't going back to Aunt Lattie's. She stormed off and said, "Well, stay here with your crack addict mother then!" I watched Star walked down the front steps and then those same two ladies from the school walked off the porch with her. I knew their next move would be in the house. I ran through all floors of the house looking for my momma. One of my cousins told me she was in one of the bedrooms on the third floor. Knocking on the door, I yelled over and over, "Momma, DYFS is here to take me with them! Please come out and tell them I'm with you." After a few moments, my mother opened the door and yelled in my face, "Well, go with them then, shit!" My heart sank so low I couldn't feel a thing. It was as if time stood still for a moment. My two godbrothers looked at me like I was a wounded dog. I turned away and walked slowly down the stairs to the DYFS car.

When I got in the car, the two ladies were nice. They said things like, "You did the right thing sweetheart. I know you want to be with your brother and sister. I want you to know you're brave for making such a mature decision." However, Star said some hurtful things. "Why you acting so stupid, Sheenah? You know Momma don't want us, why you keep pestering and following her? Just let her smoke her crack and die!" I didn't feel like Star felt. I wanted my momma. I wanted to be with her. I didn't care how many drugs she took, she was my mother. But I was angry too! Angry because drugs had made my mother love them more than me. How could she sing those beautiful songs to me and not love me? How could she hug me so tight that I feel like a part of her, and she doesn't care where I might spend the night or who might get to hurt me? How could she, how could she, how could she? I was extremely mad all over again, and then we arrived at Aunt Lattie's house.

As soon as I got out the car, Riana was walking up to me saying, "My mother don't want you. She gonna tell DYFS to take you and Jihaad and Star gonna stay with us. Y'all going to a foster home." One of the workers held my hand up the stairs to Aunt Lattie's apartment. I saw Delores' old backdoor first. My hands started to shake. The closer we got to Aunt Lattie's door, the more my body shook. The worker directed the other woman up the stairs with Star and Riana. "Calm down baby, it's gonna be okay," she said to me in a calm voice as she rubbed the side of my shoulder. All I could do was shake my head "no" profusely. The lady started to look worried. "Oh my God, sweetie do you need to see a doctor?" Now she was shaking too. I felt like I was going to fall, so I took off running down the back steps instead. "Wait!" yelled the middle aged black woman. At the corner, I thought about turning back but my feet said, "Keep going, Sheenah." I walked around the city a little while before I worked up the nerve to go back to Aunt Lattie's house. When I knocked on the front door and announced myself, Riana opened it and said, "My mother said go to your room and don't come out until she tells you to." Shortly after that, Star brought me a dinner plate and after I ate it, Riana told me to go take a bath. I went to sleep by myself that night. Aunt Lattie would kick me out again before my tenth birthday.

The next morning, I forgot about what Aunt Lattie said and headed to the bathroom. In the middle of the hallway, my aunt yelled for me to go back in the room. That day, all the kids did everything before me. I was last to eat, go to school, the bathroom, and bathe. It was like that for about two weeks. Then one day after Aunt Lattie went grocery shopping, she ordered for me to come down and carry the bags upstairs. After the third trip up, I realized none of the other kids were helping. Jihaad noticed the look on my face and went back down to help me. "Go your ass back upstairs, boy." my aunt said to my little brother. Before I knew it, my mouth flew open. "Why he can't help me? Why are none of the other kids carrying these bags?!" She raised her hand and slapped me across my face. I took off running up the stairs and when she got up the stairs, she told me to go stand in the pantry. "No!" I screamed out. "If you don't, I'm gonna get my belt and beat your little ass!" my aunt yelled back. I stood in the floor with my fists clenched. Aunt Lattie took off her belt and charged toward me. My only thought was to keep her from hitting me with the belt. She hit me with the belt a few times before I could get it from her grasp. When I did, I started to hit her with the belt. When I realized what I was doing, my aunt fell against the kitchen chairs. "Get the fuck out and don't ever come back!" she yelled while throwing articles of food from the bags that were now on the floor.

This time, I only stayed gone a few days. I went to my great grandparents' house again and they told me there that my mom had been locked up on an assault charge. I wasn't sure what that meant at the time, but I still didn't want to chance going back to Aunt Lattie's. My godmother let me sleep in the room with Mumin, but I never really got to see her (since she was nursing a drug habit too). Hank wasn't around because my momma was in jail, so that meant no extra dollars for food. I was wearing the same clothes everyday this time, 'cause when my aunt told me to leave, I left everything—even my doll. I missed that doll every night when it was time to go to sleep.

I didn't go to school either. I knew the DYFS would be waiting to catch me there. On the second night of my stay, one of my great uncles beat his girlfriend up really bad in the basement. She called the police and when they came, they basically cleared out anyone who didn't "live" there. As soon as they went in the second floor apartment, I went down the back step and hid in my great grandfathers grape vine in the backyard. When I felt like the cops weren't paying attention, I snuck off the block and headed toward the bar around the corner to look for Hank to get some money for food.

When I crossed the bridge, I noticed a man pulling on this lady. She was obviously drunk or something and she didn't seem to want to go with him. He was yelling and cursing at her, calling her bitches and skeezers and whores. She was crying and begging him to stop. I decided to follow them because I felt so bad for the lady. He started shoving the lady down a dark side street and telling her to come on with him or he would "knock her motherfucking ass out." She started yelling, "Why you always wanna try and beat on me when nobody could see you?" "You're a punk bitch, that's why—you pussy!" The man got so mad he started dragging the woman. As he was dragging her, she was fighting and yelling back to him. Then he yanked her disoriented body behind a truck. I hid between some cars and listened to the two scuffle for a few moments. I could hear the woman's moans and groans grew short and more faint. The man yelled, "Get up! Get up, bitch!" I didn't hear the lady's voice at all. The man struck out and ran down the street looking behind him. I didn't see the lady so I walked a little closer to the truck. Looking toward the bumper of the car parked ahead, I could see the tips of her shoes, but I didn't see or hear her moving. I was afraid to look at her face so, I ran back toward the bar.

There were a lot of people in front of the bar, but none of them seemed to know Hank. I was still shook up from the incident with the man and lady, so I headed back toward my great grandparents' house. All the doors were locked, so I slept on the porch. Before dosing off, the image of the tanned skinned woman laying lifelessly on the ground flashed across my mind continually. I knew then that I would never let that happen to me, no matter what! In the morning, there was a blanket over me and a note tucked under my shoulder that read:

Dear Sheenah,

> *I know you want to be with your mom, but she's not well and the streets is no place for a little girl. I wish I could take you with me but me and my son don't have nowhere to go either. I love you and I want you to go back to Aunt Lattie's house. If you need me, I'm always here for you.*

> *Love,*
> *Aunt Yolanda*

I sat on the porch and cried. Then I got up and went back to Aunt Lattie's house. When I got there, she just looked at me through the screen door and said. "Go wash your ass, I don't know where you been. With your little grown ass! Come eat your breakfast and go back to the room. You can't go to school, you can't do nothing else either." When the kids got out of school, my sister and brother came in the room and Star acted like she didn't even see me. Jihaad's face lit up like always and we sat on the floor and talked a while. He told me about how mean everyone was treating him while I was gone. He told me how my aunt's husband had been making him take off his shoes and massage his feet. That really disturbed me, so I started making Jihaad hang around me all the time, just so I could keep him safe.

I was having trouble sleeping now, so I spent a lot of time looking out the window at night. The corner had gotten very busy over the year and it was one very particular detail I would always pay attention to when the sun went down. Her name was Holly. She was a drug dealer. She had a drug dealer boyfriend too and every night, I would observe her making sales. People would be begging her for the drugs sometimes. She was emotionless. Of all the times I'd seen her (during the day or through the window), she would never smile. I admired her because she always seemed to be in control.

Aunt Lattie had gotten really sick and went in the hospital two days before my tenth birthday. Uncle Carl was home more regularly this time. One evening, he asked Jihaad to take his boots off in front of me. My brother just looked at me. I started laughing and stood to my feet! Holding Jihaad's hand I said, "He ain't taking off your shoes today or any other day. Don't ask him to do that ever again." My uncle Carl just stared in shock, but at that very moment, I could tell he respected me. Soon after that, I started getting into even more fights. I would fight in school, the neighborhood, on outings—you name it. It got to the point that nobody wanted to watch me or be my friend, so I spent a lot of time on punishment, locked away in that little room, looking out of the window. It seemed like my punishments would get extremely strict whenever my aunt was home from the hospital. The spring before I went to sixth grade would be a time I would never forget. My mom had come home from jail (for the umpteenth time) and started to come and see us more frequently at Aunt Lattie's house. My aunt was in and out of the hospital and my mom and uncle started to "hang out" a lot. My uncle's birthday had come and my cousin Riana had given him a small birthday gathering with a cake. All of the kids of the house attended. My mother was the only other adult. Momma was high on some type of drug because she was acting strange and her eyes looked really weird. She paid a lot of attention to Star that night. She kept bossing her around and yelling at her. She even threatened to beat Star if she didn't "listen to what she was told." Right after we'd sung happy birthday, Riana went to cut the cake. My momma insisted that Star cut the cake because she was the "oldest" in the house. Out of nowhere, my sister told my mother to mind her business. My mother rushed toward my sister and started screaming in her face. "Swap!' My sister swung and slapped my mother and they began to fight. I looked on in horror as my cousins and uncle looked on in amazement. My brother was screaming and crying so I took the initiative and did the best I could to break them up. Taking kicks, punches, and scratches, it got easier when Uncle Carl started to help me. We managed to separate my mother and my sister. When we finally pried Star off my mother, she looked instantly sober and hurt, but not my sister! She was screaming and calling my mom all kinds of names. "You're not my mother! You don't even love us! All you wanna do is get high! I hate you, bitch! Get outta my life! Sheenah can have you, I don't want you to be my mother no more!" Uncle Carl and Riana tried all they could to keep my sister from charging at my mother again. Finally, my mother left the apartment sobbing all the way down the back steps.

Uncle Carl and my mother's relationship would turn sour very soon. Before the summer season could end, Aunt Lattie was back in the hospital and Momma and Uncle Carl started "hanging out" again. Then Uncle Carl was missing some money, ironically the same week my mom was at the house "babysitting." They got into an argument and Uncle Carl called my mother a crack head. My mother returned the insult. "If I'm a crack head, then you're one right along with me 'cause we both get high! You just do a better job at hiding your shit!" Riana looked like she'd seen a ghost! Uncle Carl called my mother a liar and threw her out of the house.

It was the end of the summer now and Aunt Lattie had come home and gone in the hospital again. A few weeks later, Uncle Carl had beaten Jihaad for wasting food. I was out in the streets with some of the neighborhood kids when it happened. The next day, he beat him again for not cleaning the room (again I wasn't there). Later that night, he beat Jihaad for 'talking back' to him. I was there for this beating. I still don't know why I didn't help my brother that day. But I was glad that he stood up for himself. In the middle of the beating, he yelled out, "I'm leaving this house!" and ran out the door. Later on that night, Jihaad showed up at the front door accompanied by my mother. When the door opened, my mother jumped on Uncle Carl instantly. They were fighting all through the house, breaking things and everything. When the fight was over, my mom spit in Uncle Carl's face, took Jihaad's hand and left the apartment. The next day, Aunt Lattie came home from the hospital.

As soon as Aunt Lattie got in the backdoor, she called for me and my sister. "Star, get on the phone with your grandmother and see when she gone be picking y'all up. Y'all can't stay here no more." My grandmother talked to Star, Aunt Lattie then talked me. The message was clear. Aunt Lattie was getting rid of us and Mah Mah didn't really want to keep us either.

CHAPTER 5

The ride to Mah Mah's house in the suburbs seemed longer that day. I'd been there before and each time, the ride seemed longer than the previous. Maybe the silence in her husband's car made it longer this time. In any event, we were going, obviously against her husband's will. Uncle Phillip had been living there since his recent break up with his girlfriend, following the birth of his first daughter, and Uncle Mike would stay there from time to time when he wasn't running the streets or locked up. Mah Mah had devised a plan for my uncles to take custody of us and move us to another apartment in the city by way of our public assistance. Uncle Phillip instantly agreed, but Uncle Mike was hesitant because he didn't really want the responsibility of caring for three kids. A few days later, Mah Mah and her husband took all of us back to the city to look for my momma. When we found her, she was walking down Park Avenue toward my great grandparents' house. When she saw the car, she looked at it as though she didn't want to be bothered. She was obviously high. Mah Mah jumped out the car and yelled to my mom, "You need to come and get your kids, Mona! They're your responsibility and ain't nobody else got no room for them. I can't keep taking care of your kids. I got my own life now." My grandmother and mother got into a screaming match right there on the corner. Then my momma stormed away from Mah Mah. My uncles followed after her and returned shortly saying, "She don't want these kids Mah. We just gon have to take care of them." While riding back to Mah Mah's house, I thought to myself, "Momma didn't even speak to us. When Jihaad called her, she didn't even look at him. Maybe she really don't want us. Maybe she don't love us. Maybe everybody else is right, my mother loves drugs more than us."

The following month, my uncles had joint custody of us and we were moving into a two family house in a new town. The owners of the house, an old man and his wife, lived on the first floor and their daughter and her five children lived in the basement. Her kids were bad and her second oldest son was a bully. Me and Jihaad were afraid of him, so we spent a lot of time playing in the house. Living there was very lonely. We were away from all of our family members (which was something we weren't used to) and the apartment was roach infested. We even went through periods when they would cut off our cold water. I remember during the summer that year, the owners cut off the cold water and we had to flush the toilet by dumping buckets of hot water down the toilet and if we did it too much in one day, the toilet would back up and the whole apartment would smell like feces. After being at this apartment about four months, my momma would come and spend some night with us, telling us how much she loved us and that she let my uncles take care of us because she "wasn't well." A few days before my mother came to the apartment, Uncle Phillip went to rehab. Before then, I didn't know he even used drugs. He always seemed normal around us. He always made jokes with us and played music like everyone else in our family. He would occasionally get up on Saturday mornings and make breakfast, so I had no reason to think he was an addict. By age eleven, I knew that if a person had to go to rehab it meant they had a drug problem. I guess this was why I was so confused at my mother telling us she wasn't well enough to take care of us. Uncle Mike was using drugs when he took custody of us and he still was able to manage . . . I guess.

Anyway, before Uncle Phillip went to the rehab, he and Tina had their second child, a boy named Ikey, and Tina and her three kids, my two little cousins, and her oldest son had moved in. The day Uncle Phillip came home from rehab, he told us he had a new girlfriend and she was going to be moving in. Tina got up from the table, packed her bags, and had her sisters to come and move her out. She was quiet all the way until her sisters came through the door. When they got all her stuff out, she started beating Uncle Phillip across the head and throwing things at him saying, "How could you do this to your family, Phil. You're wrong, Phil! I hate you, Phil." Her sisters finally got her off my uncle and off the premises before the old people downstairs could call the police. Within a couple of hours, Uncle Phillip's new girlfriend, Diane, was moving in with her three kids.

Diane was pretty, short, medium built woman with skin like mine and glasses. She had two sons; Mark, who was about a year older than me, and Stevie who was two years younger than Jihaad. Stevie had a deformed ear and he was often defensive about anyone staring or making remarks about it. Cynthia was her baby girl. She was only six years old when they moved in. She was sneaky and liked to steal all the time. Whenever she would get caught, she would blame it on her brother Stevie and somehow, he would get in trouble even if he wasn't found to be guilty. Star hated them living with us, so she spent a lot of time in our room away from everybody. The only times she would emerge was when Diane started cooking. Diane was a good cook and she always made sure food was in the house. Uncle Mike would always spend the money from our checks on drugs and his "business" so Diane would buy food for the entire house with her own public assistance. It didn't take long before Uncle Phillip stared spending more time across town with Tina and his kids. Whenever he did come home, he would make jokes and before long, Diane became the bunt of them. They didn't seemed to be getting along that much after Uncle Phillip brought his family to the house to stay for the weekend. In that weekend, Cynthia told Uncle Phillip's daughter Mia that he was her daddy too. Mia questioned her father about this very tearfully. When Uncle Phillip told us about it, we knew he and Diane's relationship was pretty much over.

One night on the first of the month, Diane and Uncle Mike went food shopping and brought home a lot of food. All the kids in the house were so happy! It was so much food that Diane had to store some of it in the closet near the top porch. That night we ate a big dinner, had ice cream, snacks, and lots of soda. When Uncle Phillip came home, he was drunk. Diane started to talk about how drunk he was and said that he was no longer in recovery because he had gotten drunk. Uncle Phillip immediately started calling Diane all kinds of names. He called her stupid for moving in with a man she had met at a rehab and commented on how she had no sexual discretion. Diane first started to cry and when she did, her oldest son, Mark, took a swing at Uncle Phillip. He grabbed the boy to stop him from landing the punch and then Diane followed suit in an attempt to assault him. Once Uncle Phillip moved Mark out the way, he and Diane were in a full fledged fight! Uncle Mike rushed in from the back room to see what was happening. When he saw Uncle Phillip grabbing Diane, he jumped in the fight! Now, Diane and Uncle Mike were jumping at Uncle Phillip! This was the first time I'd ever seen my uncles fight. My momma and my aunt would fight all the time and while we didn't like it, it didn't surprise us. The whole time of the fight between my uncles, Uncle Phillip was yelling, "You gon fight me over a bitch man?! I'm your brother!" He yelled out about Diane being a nasty whore and a home wrecker too. He said that she wasn't worth a dime and that she would have sex with anybody. After the police came and had Uncle Phillip to spend the night somewhere else, which he did with no problem, Uncle Mike and Diane sat all the kids of the house down and told us that they were now in a relationship.

Prayer
Who am I to be?
When violence is all I see?
Closed fists, bruised wrists.
Red teeth, swelled lips.
Black and blues are now become minor scars.
I don't flinch when they swing.
I duck and post up.
Defenses.
Ready for battle, groomed for conflict, fashioned for war.
Vagabond!
Leather!
Back down—Never!

Quarrel is my second skin.
For all I know is violence!

It was very strange for us to go from seeing Diane come out of Uncle Phillip's room to seeing her come out of Uncle Mike's room. Star called her a whore too and even started to refuse to eat her cooking. Jihaad didn't seem to care, and me, I was just torn. I knew what she was doing was wrong, but I didn't want to judge her because I thought she might stop letting us eat the food she bought and cooked, and aside from what she'd done, I liked her okay. I guess you could say she really got on my good side. When you go from going without food, to eating when someone "feels" like feeding you and eating on the run literally, you learn to appreciate when you could eat with ease. Going to school became hard too. When I first got to the sixth grade class, I had a fight the first day. Then Coby came to my class. As soon as the teacher seated him behind me, I knew I would have a problem. He was short, stocky, light-skinned, and he intimidated me the moment I laid eyes on him. He first would tease me on bathroom breaks and then again after lunch. Then he would just tease me after school and follow me home. Whenever I walked home with one of the kids from the neighborhood, he wouldn't bother me, but that didn't happen all the time, so he would often catch me by myself and harass me. One day after school, the whole sixth grade followed me home because Coby told them he was going to punch me in the face. My classmates were sure I was going to fight back, but that day after school, Coby punched me in the face and I didn't fight him back.

That night, I cried myself to sleep thinking about how many kids saw him hit me and thought they could do the same thing to me. My pride was hurt! I was embarrassed. The next morning, my mother came to the house and I stayed home from school. By this time in my life, no one was placing demands for us to go to school. It was almost optional. It really didn't make a difference to me anyway since now, my grades were horrible. At about lunch time, Diane came to my room door and told me to follow her. "I know why you didn't want to go to school today. The kids down the street told me what happened. Here, I want you to carry this with you tomorrow." Diane handed me a razor blade trimmed in a blue plastic protector. She said, "If that boy put his hands on you tomorrow, cut his ass too short to shit and run home as fast as you can." I smiled and tucked the blade in my pocket. Suddenly, I wasn't scared anymore! I went back to my room to watch television, occasionally pulling the razor from my pocket. Then I thought, "What if I cut myself trying to cut Coby?" I went back to feeling helpless again.

When my sister came home, she asked me to walk with her to the store. All the kids from the neighborhood teased me about Coby punching me in the face. Uncle Mike had already called for my cousin Ali to come and beat him up and Mark wasn't there when Coby punched me so he wasn't punished for not defending me. When we got back to the house, the sun was going down and my momma was standing on the top porch. "Sheenah, get your ass up here," she said like she was going to beat me once I got up the stairs. I took my time getting to the top porch and when I did, my momma was sitting on a milk crate smoking a cigarette. "What happened at school yesterday?" I looked down and tears fell from my eyes. Momma sprang up from the crate! "See how you feel right now?! Don't you EVER let no fucking body make you feel like this, you hear me girl?!" "Yes." I said, flinching from my mother standing over me. "NO, she shouted! You can't be this scared in this life!" Then she calmed down and lifted my chin again. "Is this why you fight people all the time, Sheenah, 'cause you scared?" I never gave her an answer. She folded her arms in front of me and said, "I'm gon' teach you something you better not ever forget." My mother pulled a switch blade and a razor from each side of her bra and gave me my first "cutting" lesson. She showed me everything from "jacking up" to "getting a release." I went to school with confidence the next day.

For the next few weeks, Coby didn't bother me, but that didn't stop the kids in school from talking about how he had "snuck" me weeks prior. Then one day at lunchtime, he walked up to me and told me he was going to whoop my ass afterschool. This time, he didn't pass it around the school, so I knew that meant he was planning to really give me a beating that no one could attempt to stop. I spent seventh and eight periods reviewing everything my momma taught me. When the bell rung, I walked to my locker, hoping I wouldn't have to use none of those techniques. When I walked out the school yard, Coby was waiting for me at the corner. I walked as slow as I could to get away from the crowd, in an effort to keep me from potentially being embarrassed again. As soon as I turned the corner, Coby and another boy started following me. I put my hands in my pocket on the blue razor I'd gotten from Diane. I felt him get closer to me and I clicked the razor once and looked back. He and his friend jogged up closer to me and I clicked the razor a second time. "Yeah, this should be enough." I thought as my fingertips grazed the side of the blade and I gripped it tight in my hand. Then he pushed me and I stumbled. With my hand still gripping the razor I said, "You better leave me alone if you know like I know." Coby took a swing at my face and as I ducked my head, he rushed me and grabbed me into a headlock. He was shorter than me so my entire face was to the ground. I pulled out the razor with one hand and held Coby around the waist with the other. I shut my eyes and started yelling as the razor hit him across the face and arms over and over. When he realized what I was doing, he let my neck go and started screaming too. When I realized the whole afterschool crowd was watching, Coby was on the ground covering his face and I was on top of him swinging the razor across his hands and arms like a cheetah. A girl belted a piercing scream from the crowd and I instantly got scared. In a panic, I sprung from the ground and ran all the way home. When I got to the porch and rang the bell, I couldn't find the razor! I hid at the back of one of the houses until all the commotion died down and I went to search for my missing blade. I later found it lying in the street on the corner. I sprinted from where the incident happened earlier. I knew I'd gotten "sloppy' like Momma warned me against. When I finally got home, Diane and Momma were waiting for me on the top porch. Momma ran down to meet me and as she took the razor from my shaking hands, she told me not to worry and that Hank was coming to get me before the police came and as soon as Hank pulled up, so did the police. They asked my uncles' questions as my momma and Diane paced the living room floor. Jihaad was holding my hand and Star was standing in the doorway shaking her head. The police then put handcuffs on me and put me in the squad car. I just turned eleven-years-old.

When I got to the station, a police woman told me I was being charged with assault and weapon possession. Thankfully, I didn't kill Coby. He only had some abrasions to his face, head and arms as the police described it, but his mother wanted to press charges to the fullest extent. I ended up spending a few hours in the juvenile precinct and being released with the notification of a court date to follow. The next day, I was pulled out of class in the morning and suspended for five days for bringing a weapon to school. This was the beginning of my many charges to follow.

CHAPTER 6

We had been living with my uncles for a little under a year now and Uncle Phillip had moved out months ago with Tina. Uncle Mike and Diane were still going together and both were now back to using drugs. They'd stay up half the night running in and out of the apartment to buy and use heroin. Uncle Mike would do a lot of nodding when he was high and Diane would do a lot of talking. I would be the only kid that would listen to her long stories and most of the time, she would keep me up well past my bedtime. The roaches in the apartment were bad now since the people on the first floor bombed their apartment. The kitchen would swarm with roaches when the lights were out and it became common to have to dust them off you after coming in the front door. When summer came, we were out of cold water for over a month and the toilet was not working so the house always had a stench of feces and urine. With no air conditioning in the apartment, the smell seemed to be stagnant and ten times worse. Diane tried to always keep it neat and Uncle Mike burned incenses all day to try and drown out the smell. But if you've been in a place with a foul smell you know the worst thing you can do is put a sweet smell on top of it. We all had grown immune to it, but we would never invite our friends over to visit. Aunt Yolanda and Ali had started to visit more and more once she got a job working at the college, and Mah Mah's visits became less and less. Aunt Yolanda would come over and give me and my siblings' money, and even bring sanitary items for my sister. I hadn't yet gotten my period so she would buy me bras, tee shirts, and socks to wear. I had pretty much developed into a full-fledged tomboy, and sharing a room with Star had become a task. I went from braids as a six year old to ponytails and bangs as a nine year old, to French braids, sneakers, and baggy jeans everyday as an eleven year old. Living at Aunt Lattie's, Star and Ruby would paint their nails and wear dresses. I was never interested. As I began to get older, I saw femininity as a weakness so I did all I could to make myself masculine. I would wear my cousin Ali's sneakers and tee shirts and run with boys all afternoon. I had always had boys for friends but now I was starting to look like one too. No earrings, lip gloss, or fancy jackets, I was rough and extremely angry.

Right before we were kicked out of the apartment, I had a run with the boy downstairs me and Jihaad had been afraid of since we'd moved in. I was leaving the corner store and he was out front waiting to tease and torment me. I wasn't afraid, so when I looked him in the face, I just turned and walked by him. He started to follow me and before I let him get too close up behind me, I turned around and started swinging my fists. After landing maybe three punches to his face, he started to run from me. When I realized I was chasing him, the bag I was holding was gone and I was a few feet away from the front porch. The boy downstairs had sprinted toward the backyard and down the basement steps. There was a boy standing on the porch next door. He called out to me saying, "Hey! Fast as he was running, I didn't know somebody that pretty was chasing him." The two teenagers on the porch with him began to laugh and proceeded up the steps to the apartment. "Hey what's your name?" said the brown skinned boy with light brown eyes who looked about my same age. "Sheenah." I said still walking in the front door. Once the door slammed behind me, a few fast knocks followed. I turned around and saw the boys smiling and waving at me as I stood in the middle of the stairway looking back at him. I smiled and kept walking up the stairs thinking out loud, "he is so cute."

The day we left the apartment for good was the day before the constable came to lock the door. Uncle Mike kept rushing us to get all our clothes down the stairs to Mah Mah husband's trunk. We didn't have much, so we were all able to fit our stuff in there. A few minutes before we got in the car, the boy with the light brown eyes was crossing the street toward me with another boy. He smiled all the way across the street and I just watched him thinking, "What is he smiling at?" "Hey, Sheenah, I been waiting to see you again. Why you didn't come back out that day to talk to me?" I sighed and looked at him saying, "I don't even know your name." "Well, ask me! I asked you your name!" he exclaimed. I rolled my eyes and turned my head. He stood there for a few more minutes asking me to ask him what his name was but I never did. Mah Mah came down the stairs yelling, "Y'all kids get in the car so we can go, I'm glad y'all outta this piece of shit!" The boy looked shocked! "Y'all moving?" he said. I nodded my head and looked away. As I walked away, he touched my shoulder and said, "My name is Selah. Don't ever forget me, okay?"

This time, Mah Mah had different plans for where we would stay until Uncle Mike found another apartment. She took us to Uncle Phillip's house on the south side. By this time Uncle Phillip and Tina had three kids between the two of them and another on the way. In only a two bedroom apartment, sleeping arrangements were difficult. Like in the beginning at Aunt Yolanda's house, Jihaad slept with Tina's oldest son on one mattress, and me and Star slept on the box spring in the same room. It didn't take me long to discover that Star was Tina's favorite over me and Jihaad had fit in perfectly since she had a son for him to play with. Again, I was the outcast. I kept a low profile at Uncle Phillip's. He was always at work so I never really felt completely comfortable there. I kept quiet and did as I was told. Somehow, I always put Tina in a bad mood. She was always angry when I was around, so I spent a lot of time roaming the neighborhood and sitting alone in the back room, writing songs, raps, and poems. Sometimes I would write about Selah too (since he told me not to forget him). I was never brave enough to let anyone read them because they were all mainly my private thoughts. I kept them in a composition book I bought from the school store and it was almost full when we moved in with Uncle Phillip and Tina. There was a girl in the neighborhood named Tye and I would follow her around because everybody called her a tomboy. She wore baggy jeans and big tee shirts just like me, only hers were always clean and sporty. Her boots and jackets were nice too, but she wore her hair in a ponytail with bangs. She never knew I was following her, but I became curious about where she was going every day with a book bag and a plastic school bag (since she didn't go to school). One evening, right before I turned twelve, I found out what she was doing. I had followed her to a three family house a couple of blocks away and when she went up the stairs, this time I went up them too. On the second floor, a guy let her in and she handed him the book bag. He opened it and pulled out a plastic bag full of reefer, which was now called weed. Hiding behind the banister, I saw her hand him the plastic bag too and he pulled out another plastic bag full of plastic baggies. The guy handed her a lot of money and they never even said anything to each other. Tye counted her money and left the building. Following behind her, I realized I had just witnessed a girl sell a lot of drugs.

Tina would leave the house occasionally, taking my sister Star with her to pan handle for money at different shopping center lots and while that happened, all the rest of the kids would run around the house while Uncle Phillip slept. He worked nights so most of the day he would sleep. Tina's son would be at school and me and Jihaad would be at the house with the two smaller kids. I would change diapers, warm bottles, and rock them to sleep until their mother came home with money she never shared with us. Then one afternoon, my mother came to visit. She sat and talked with Uncle Phillip and Tina, and Tina asked her when she was coming to get the three of us. Before she answered, she looked around at all three of us and said, "I'm working on that now. Soon, though." Before she left, she told Jihaad to walk her down the stairs. I tried to follow but she ordered me to go back up the stairs. That day, I felt like my mother really didn't want to be bothered with me. Her hugs to her other children were longer that day. Her conversation about me to Tina was shorter too. I didn't know why, but I knew in my heart something was wrong.

The next day, I followed my routine of roaming the neighborhood to watch the hustlers in action and when I returned to the apartment, Jihaad was gone. I asked Uncle Phillip where he was and he told me my mom came and got him. "Where did they go? Why didn't she take me and Star? Is she coming back to get us?" This was the first time I actually verbalized to anyone these questions that often lurked in my head. All Uncle Phillip did was shrug his shoulders and walk to the back of the apartment. After a few weeks, I accepted that my momma wasn't coming back to get me and Star. When she first came to get Jihaad, it didn't really seem to bother Star, but after a week or two, Star stopped wanting to go with Tina to beg for money from strangers. That's when Tina began being mean to the both of us.

Living at Uncle Phillip and Tina's house was a little different from living in the last apartment. At the last place, we lived with a lot of roaches, on the south side, we lived with a lot of rodents. Starr and I would sleep on the box spring on the floor and some nights, the mice would be brave enough to get on the box spring and climb on us to try and suck our drool while we were sleeping. One night we took turns staying up to keep the mice from the box spring while the other would sleep. We did that until morning light when the mice wouldn't feel confident about roaming the apartment. We must've really got on Tina's nerves because when she came back from taking her son to school, she woke me and Star up and told us, "Y'all get up and go find your mother. Y'all can't stay here anymore."

Me and Star got up and dressed. We didn't say anything to each other until we got out of the apartment. She looked at me and I looked at her. Then she said, "It's too far to walk all the way over there. Let's just go to Aunt Yolanda's house." Neither one of us had any money so calling her house was out of the question, so we walked about five miles to Aunt Yolanda's. When we got there, we'd just missed her. "She just left for work, but y'all can stay here til she comes home," said my aunt's boyfriend, Randy. No one in the family liked him because he would always beat Aunt Yolanda up and sometimes beat Ali as well. "Here, y'all can stay in Ali's room up on the third level and I'll call your aunt soon and let her know y'all here." Me and Star went up the stairs and Ali was just about to leave for school. "Hey y'all! My mom gon be so happy ya'll here! How long y'all gon stay with us? Where's Jihaad?" Neither me nor Star answered his questions, instead we let him do all the talking and we just smiled and nodded our heads. Before he left, he brought us up some breakfast from the kitchen and told us he'd be back before two. By now, Ali was scarce at school and in and out of trouble in the neighborhood. He walked down the stairs and slam locked the door behind him. The room stayed silent until Star and I drifted off to sleep to the sound of the television. After sleeping for a few hours, I woke up to an empty room. I went down the stairs and searched the entire house. The house was empty and Star was gone.

When my aunt came home from work, she was so happy to see me. She hugged me really tight and asked me tons of questions. After trying to answer them all, she asked me if I was in school. "No," I said, hanging my head low. "What! What grade are you in?" she said. "I'm in the seventh grade. I think I passed the sixth last year." "That's a damn shame," said my aunt, "somebody need to get you in school, niecy."

Of all the questions Aunt Yolanda asked me that day, she never asked me where my mother was or if I even wanted to go to her. I guess she knew what I'd finally discovered. Momma was fully wrapped into her drug life. My aunt kept all her statements and questions about me and that made me feel special. She told me I would be staying with her for a while and that she would take good care of me. She cooked before she left for work every day. She even bought me new clothes and underwear and made sure I kept them clean. She even permed what little hair I had left now and fixed it really nice for me. Living with Aunt Yolanda was always different from living anywhere else. Unlike being at Aunt Lattie's, I never had to get permission to go in the refrigerator or go to the bathroom. Aunt Yolanda always treated me like I was her own child. She didn't make me feel like a visitor and this time, Ali was barely home because he'd started selling drugs. When he was around, he treated me like the sister he'd never had.

After making me look decent again, she looked down at my feet and asked me how long I'd had my shoes. "Aunt Lattie gave me these shoes from her thrift store when we first moved there." I answered. Aunt Yolanda sat me down and placed my foot in her lap discovering one big hole in the toe of each shoe and the loose soles. "You mean to tell me you been wearing these shoes for two years?" she said with a heartbroken look in her eyes. "I had some other sneakers, but they went missing when we moved from the last apartment." I said trying to make my aunt feel better. "Well, I'm calling Mah Mah to see if she could help me get you some new shoes." Aunt Yolanda said, dropping my feet to the ground and pulling me into her for a hug.

Because Mah Mah lived far out from the city and couldn't make it to Aunt Yolanda's until the weekend to bring me the money for the shoes, the morning she was to come, Aunt Yolanda gave me a five dollar bill to take the bus to the shoe store and told me to make sure I got a good pair of sneakers to practice my running in. Ali stayed at the house with me that Saturday while I waited around for Mah Mah. As soon as she pulled up with her husband, Aunt Yolanda kissed my cheek and said, "Later, Sheenah. Mah Mah don't like me no more." I didn't ask any questions, I just walked up to the car and kissed my grandmother. "I got to get to bingo, but here go thirty dollars to get you some shoes. That's all I have so make the best of it." I thanked Mah Mah and she kissed me and told me she knew I would be okay. Before the tears rolled down her face, her husband pulled away from the curb. I sat there confused for a minute then proceeded to the bus stop.

The bus took so long to come that I started to walk to the plaza on my own. I walked through two cities to get to the shoe store because I always heard that things were cheaper near the upper suburbs. I sang the whole entire trip! Most of the time, I was singing now because I had discovered singing would always make me feel better. I sung everything! My emotions, thoughts, and things I wanted to happen. When I wasn't singing, I was talking to God. I don't think it made me feel any better, it just made me feel good that somebody was actually listening to me. When I finally got to the shoe store, I bought a pair of black sneakers. That was the first time I'd purchased any article of clothing or shoes on my own. I was so happy that once I paid the cashier, I trashed the old shoes and wore the new ones out of the store. On my walk to the bus stop to head back to Aunt Yolanda's, I thought about what Mah Mah said about knowing that I would be okay. Then, that small voice inside spoke to me and said, "Go to your old neighborhood." No matter what I did to ignore that voice, I just couldn't drown it out. Before I knew it, I'd passed the bus stop and walked all the way across town, two and a half blocks from the building I grew up in.

CHAPTER 7

My family was now in the process of selling the building since my great grandparents had both died a few years prior. Still all the tenants were family, and as I walked down the street toward the building, several of my family members greeted me with hugs, "heys," and kisses. As I proceeded across the street to enter the building, my mother came running down the steps toward me screaming, "What the fuck are you doing all the way over here? Who told you to come here? Who sent you over here?" "Momma, why you leave me?" I said with my hands stretched out toward her. Then behind her comes Jihaad. I looked at him and she looked back at me like he shared her sentiments. While my mother was still yelling, Star came in the door behind me. I turned and looked at Star, then at Momma, then Jihaad and they all looked directly at me. "You can't stay here!" Ain't no room for you over here! Go back to Yolanda's house!" she shouted. "Momma, what about me? I'm your child too! I thought you loved me! How you just take them and leave me? You don't love me?" I went on and on while sobbing and flopping down on the steps as people passed in and out of the hallway doors. Then my mother just walked passed me. As I sat on the steps crying, I started to hear a commotion from outside. I sprang up from the step and out of the hallway to find Momma and Hope (my godmother) in the street getting ready to fight. "Bitch, you don't tell her she can't stay here! You get the fuck out, bitch! She got a place to sleep before the fuck you do!" My family members broke up the argument and my godmother walked directly to me and said, "You ain't gotta go nowhere! You can stay here just like everybody else." So that night, I called my aunt and told her I found my mother over at Aunt Hope's and that Jihaad and Star was there too. She didn't sound surprised, but didn't sound hurt when I told her I wanted to stay over at the building with them. The next day, Mumin gave me bus fare to go get my clothes and I spent the day with Aunt Yolanda and Ali before going back to the building.

It seemed Momma got used to me being at Aunt Hope's really fast. It was probably because Aunt Hope would constantly remind her that if I had to go somewhere else, she would have to go somewhere else too. Now, Aunt Hope lived in the building at the exact same apartment Delores molested me in when I was small. When I went in that first day, it crossed my mind. But I told myself, "That was then. You're eleven now. You don't have to think about that if you don't want to." Those thoughts were helping until Aunt Hope told me she wanted all the girls to sleep in that room. "I can't!" I said abruptly, cutting her off. "I don't like to sleep near kitchens with open doors!" The room was directly across from the kitchen and the room didn't have a door. "Okay, well you sleep in there with Mumin and them and if that ain't good, you can sleep in the living room with Mosse and them." "I'm gonna stay with Mumin." I said, walking down the hall to his room.

Mumin always took good care of me, so staying with him was just like sleeping with a lion at the door. No one would ever try and hurt me when he was around. He wasn't a kid that liked to fight and some might suggest that he was a bit of a scary cat, but he always got brave when it came to me. One night, he and I had a long conversation about my mom and family. I asked him if he would protect me because I always felt scared of something happening to me. Looking at me shocked, he said, "Who did something to you, Sheenah?! Tell me and I will kill them tonight! I love you, you are my little sister and if anybody ever hurt you, I'm gonna kill them." He started to get so mad that tears started welling up in his eyes. I sat up in the bed and gave my godbrother a hug saying, "I'm okay. If somebody tries to hurt me, I will tell you. I promise."

Everything that ever happened concerning the kids happened in Mumin's room. Dance contests, freestyle battles—EVERYTHING! Mumin and my older godbrother Hassan used to rap and I would sing all the hooks. The only time I would try and rap would be when only the girl children were around. They always wanted me to rap so we would spend most of the day playing beats by Marley Marl and instruments on the B sides of rap tapes. Riana and Reece would come over every day afterschool because they still lived across the hall. Whenever we got really hungry, they would bring us over to their house and let us eat with them since now, Aunt Lattie spent almost the whole year in the hospital.

By now, all the boys at Aunt Hope's house sold drugs. They even cut up their crack and bagged up their weed in Mumin's room. From drug stashes and sales, to a teenage girl's "first time' happened in Mumin's room. The grown-ups in the house were so busy getting high and looking for ways to get high that they never really had time to concentrate on what the kids of the house were or weren't doing. Aunt Hope always made a point of buying food for the house though. She had given birth to a little boy named YaYa, about two months before I came to live there. I loved to babysit him because all he did was sleep all the time. Aunt Hope gave me first priority since he was my little godbrother.

Every night, we talked ourselves to sleep. We would talk about what happened during the course of the day, who got beat for money, how many sells were made by who and all kinds of hustler's stories. Me being the only girl and the youngest in the room always made my cousins/godbrothers feel comfortable talking freely around me. The more they talked, the more I became enticed with the idea of selling drugs. But I still wasn't brave enough to try it.

One night, a couple of months before my family was due to move out of the building, Aunt Hope and Mumin got into a really big fight over some drugs that was stolen from Mumin's stash. Aunt Hope kicked Mumin out and he went to live across the hall to Aunt Lattie's house. She was still in the hospital, but figured that having Mumin in the apartment may bring some order to her household since her kids did whatever they wanted with their father in control. I began to spend a lot of days and nights over there too. Mumin was my protection from Mosse so wherever he went, he made sure that me being with him wasn't a problem. Of course, Aunt Hope didn't know I was there, but Uncle Carl didn't have a problem with me so he let me stay.

Riana and I had stayed out a little late one night and when we got back to her house, Uncle Carl was sitting in the kitchen with Aunt hope's ex husband and my alleged "godfather" Russel. As soon as he saw us, his eyes lit up. He especially paid attention to me. He rose from the chair and reached out to hug me without even speaking to me. I reluctantly hugged him back and noticed that he held me longer than I was comfortable with. He rubbed both his hands across my back and squeezed me to his chest saying, "Hey baby! I ain't seen you in years! You got so big!" I yanked away in disgust, walking past my nodding uncle at the kitchen table and into Riana's room, closing the door. When Riana came in, she was holding two can sodas asking, "Girl, what's wrong with you?" I said, "You ain't give him no hug?" She said no and went over to the radio to play a tape. Looking back at her, I instantly knew that Russel didn't do to her what he'd tried to do to me because her father was in the house. Feeling targeted again, I walked out the room and into the room with Ruby and Reece. Ruby looked at me in a way that made me instantly ill because I understood it. She looked like she was trying to be happy but she was worried. I asked her what happened and she walked toward me and grabbed both my hands and said in a whisper, "That man in there keep trying to touch me." I got furious! I was at first ashamed and afraid for myself but when I heard those words from my little cousin, I became enraged! We devised a plan to get him to chase us to Mumin's room where he was listening to loud music and putting his drugs together. We knew he defend us so we both went into the kitchen were Russel was now sitting alone. First Ruby approached him and I watched him caress her like she was a woman, rubbing his hands on the small of her back and down the side of her legs. My cousin was terrified and that's when it dawned on me that I had put too much pressure on a nine year old girl. I intervened by calling her name out and watching him scuffle across the kitchen floor like he hadn't done anything. By this time, Uncle Carl was completely passed out on the bed in Aunt Lattie's room, and Ruby had gone in there with him. Russel called me over to him and I responded. He hugged me again and then sat down in a chair and told me to sit on his lap. I said no and tried to get away from him. He grabbed me by the wrist and started to pull me to him. I was able to break away and just like I expected, he sprung up from the chair and started after me. He caught me right before I could run down the hall toward Mumin's room. This time he pulled me to him so hard, my face slammed against his chest and I could feel a bulge in his pants. As he rubbed his hands across my back and buttocks now, I wondered if I had taken this too far. "Mumin!" I called out! But the music was too loud and Uncle Carl was knocked out. I could see Ruby looking at me from her mother's bedroom doorway. Russel started trying to undo my bra through the back of my shirt and could feel my soul yelling "no" on the inside. When I finally tore away from him, I ran for my life down the hall to Mumin's room.

"Help, help, help! He's trying to get me!" I yelled, jumping in my godbrother's arms! "Who?" Mumin shouted back to me. "Russel!" I screamed again, pointing in the direction of the kitchen. Before I could tell him what happened, Mumin sprinted through the hall and down the back steps after Russel. He returned a few minutes later and I asked did he catch him. Looking disappointed, he answered no and asked me what happened. With every detail I gave him, he looked more and more frustrated and disgusted. Then the room got quiet and Ruby came in. A few moments passed and Mumin still didn't speak so Ruby left. Feeling ashamed and hurt, I started out the bedroom door. "Sheenah, you know that wasn't your fault, right?" Mumin said. I nodded yes and he said, "I still love you. I just don't wanna hug you 'cause I don't wanna scare you or make you think I'm like Russel or anybody else, but always tell me when something like that happens." I smiled at my godbrother and left the room.

When I got a chance to see my father again, it was maybe a week after the incident with Russel. Daddy came up the back steps to the building following Aunt Yolanda. When I opened the door, she yelled, "Surprise!" This was the first time I had seen my father since we lived across town with my uncles and I was so excited, I leaped into his arms. As tall as I was, he caught me and held me like I was that same five year old that use to jump in his arms when he came to visit at Mah Mah's. When I was living at Aunt Yolanda's house, we'd had some talks about my father, but I didn't think that it would result in her actually finding him and getting him to come and see me. When Star and Jihaad saw daddy, they hugged him and asked for quarters and dollars. I told my dad about the times I would try and call him at his parent's house after my momma gave me the number when I was living with Aunt Lattie, but all I kept asking him was, "Daddy, can you take me with you?" A few times he obviously ignored me, giving frequent glances across the room to Aunt Yolanda. Then, my mother came in the kitchen where we were sitting. She and daddy looked at each other like they had seen ghosts. My momma spoke to him and left the room. Then Aunt Hope came in the kitchen. "Shep, where the hell you been? I'm surprised these kids even know who you are. I hope you leaving some money here so I can feed 'em." Daddy looked angrily at Aunt Hope with his face twitching, but he never said anything to her. My eyes fell to the floor, and in that instant, I knew daddy wasn't going to take me with him.

"What's wrong, little girl?" he asked me, pulling me up from my seat. This was my opportunity to tell my daddy how scared I'd been for so long. How I needed his protection and how I felt helpless and alone. "I don't want nobody to try and get me." I blurted out before thinking! "What?" he said lifting me back into his arms! Then Mumin busted in Aunt Hope's backdoor like he had been listening to the entire conversation. "Russel was touching her. He was at Aunt Lattie's house with Carl and they were there getting high. I was in my room and Sheenah came running to me crying. I chased him out the building but I didn't catch him. If you wanna kill him, I'll help you find him!" My father squeezed me tight and I instantly got scared. He carried me out the building to his car and buckled me in the passenger seatbelt. Daddy got in the red car with his eyes looking wild and dangerous and sped off our street in a wild rage.

We drove around only a few minutes, with daddy jumping out the running car occasionally to go in a few stores and houses. The last time he jumped out the car, I saw Russel walking in the store with another man. Daddy didn't even turn off the car this time. Instead he threw the car in park, jumped out and opened his trunk. When the trunk slammed, I watched my father charge toward the store entrance and yank the door open—BAM! Within seconds, daddy was dragging Russel out the store by the back of his shirt. Looking enraged at me still sitting in the passenger's seat he yelled, "Is this him, baby?!" I slowly nodded my head in shock and watched my father beat Russel repeatedly with the iron bat he pulled from his trunk. It all seemed like a dream watching the blood run off his entire face with one side now protruding out as far up as his forehead. All I could think was "Oh my God, what have I done! My daddy is going to go to jail and it's all my fault! I shouldn't have said anything, it's not like he took my clothes off or anything!" Then I yelled, "DADDY, STOP PLEASE!" My father stopped and stared at the limp body on the cement and said to the man, "You were supposed to die today, motherfucker." Then he hocked spit on him and walked back to the car. When he got in, he pulled off calm pass the crowd of people who'd been watching the entire event. He lit a cigarette and drove over to a garage where he and I got into a different car. My father barely looked at me after he beat Russel with that bat. I couldn't help but feel embarrassed again. "What was he thinking? Was I a fresh tail girl to him too? Was I not his little girl anymore?" Maybe all of these were his feelings because when I finally looked up, we were pulling back up to the building. Daddy put the car in park and wrote a phone number on the back of a business card and told me to call him whenever I needed him. I reached over and hugged my father, he gave me a twenty dollar bill and I got out the car. Before I could open the door to the building, my dad said to me, "I love you Sheenah and don't worry I didn't kill him, okay." I gave a half smile with a huge lump in my throat and walked up the stairs to Aunt Hope's apartment, feeling abandoned again.

CHAPTER 8

When we moved from my godmother's house, it was because my uncle Michael came to get us. I guess he'd began to feel guilty for getting the welfare funds and not having us in his actual custody. Either that, or he himself needed a place to live after one of his fly by night "relationships" came to an end. Whatever the reason, Uncle Michael had come to move us in another cross town apartment. The first day we got there, none of us liked the apartment. My sister called it an abandoned house and my brother said it was creepy. I thought it was weird that it didn't have a living room or any doors. As soon as you entered, you were in a bedroom. Then you had to walk to the left and through that bedroom to get to any other room in the house. The bathroom and kitchen were at the end of this corridor and the backdoor was a metal freezer-like door, leading to a balcony and an open field for a back yard. We barely used the backdoor. We would only use it to sneak my mother in when Uncle Mike would threaten us not to let her in. It didn't take long for my uncle to find a new girlfriend. Only weeks after we all were enrolled in school did he start dating the lady upstairs. When Momma got news of her brother's dwindling interest in caring for her children, she came to the house to confront him about it. The problem was, it was the first of the month and Uncle Michael was high before the sun came up that day. When my mom asked him, "Mike, where the fuck is my kids food stamps?" he wasted no time leaping toward my mother. He first grabbed and attempted to punch her in the face. After his punches failed to land, he scooped my mother off her feet and slammed her frail body to the cement. My brother screamed and went for the ridged stick poking out of a trash can and my sister went running down the block to a pay phone to call the police. I stood there and watched my six foot, two-and-a-half inched uncle stomp my five foot-five inched mother for what seemed like an eternity. My entire body waxed hot and I couldn't hear a thing. Then, I saw a shoe fly into the air. My mother was able to interrupt his attack by snatching off her brother's shoe. Jihaad swung that stick across my uncles back and screamed until the stick broke down to a stump in his hand. When my uncle looked up and saw the look on my face, everything stopped and he fled back up the stairs to his girlfriend's house. My brother ran to embrace my mother, Star returned with the police and my mother lit a cigarette saying to the officers, "Everything is okay now officers, the man who attacked me is gone." When the cop car left, my mother made several more attempts to get my uncle to give her our food stamps at the very least. After all the stores closed, he tossed two books of the coupons out the door and my mother took us to the twenty four hour market. She bought hotdogs hamburgers, bread, cereal, milk, soda, and junk food. She cashed the rest in for cash and got high with the money.

For the next few months, my mother would be the one who would attempt to care for us. We'd go to school on a very inconsistent basis and she'd sleep while we were there. Sometimes, she wouldn't make it imperative for us to go to school, even though the schools we attended were in walking distance. When my sister Star had missed too many days to be readmitted into school without a parent, Momma shrugged it off and said, "You'll just go to a different school. Needless to say, Momma never felt like taking her and she ended up not attending school at all for the remainder of that year. Jihaad and I on the other hand, were able to continue in school that year because for us, going to school meant being able to eat more than once a day (if that). Before the school year ended that year, Star left the house one day telling us she was going for a walk. She never came back to that apartment to live. The next time we saw her was maybe a week later and she was coming to get her clothes. She and Uncle Phillip came into the apartment and announced that she would no longer be living with us and that she had been staying with him since she'd left that afternoon a week prior. My mother didn't dispute it, Uncle Michael was not aware of it (and probably didn't care anyway) and Jihaad and I just looked on as everyone around us made decisions, had opinions and voiced their feelings. The two of us just listened, looked to the ground and equally felt out casted.

It wouldn't be long from then that my mother would start to feel overwhelmed with being a parent again. Make no mistake, she did become more present in our lives, but because we were not too young that we couldn't stay home unattended, she would make her way to Aunt Hope's to hang out just about every day. The longer she stayed at the apartment with me and Jihaad, the more frequent and the longer her visits cross town would be. I remember the time after my family sold the building and Aunt Hope moved to a new apartment around the corner, she went missing for more than a week. Me and Jihaad went wild. Parties, overnight guests, breaking day, learning to really sell drugs independently—you name it, we did it! I did everything but have sex and steal, Jihaad started to do all those things and at only ten years old, he would find creative, risky, and most of the time, illegal ways to make money. I was twelve years old.

I started to rely on my little brother's schemes to feed us after the lights had been turned out only a few days after my mother left. Then one day, I came home after hanging in the neighborhood with some of the kids to discover Jihaad had left me too. I walked in his room and noticed all his shoes and toys missing. I knew for sure he wasn't coming back. The neighbors across the street told me my mom had picked him up more than an hour before I'd gotten back. I spent the remainder of the night in that dark apartment wondering why and how she could leave me again. Maybe I took too long to get back, maybe she was in a rush and her ride had to leave, maybe she was coming back to get me tomorrow. But with all the questions I asked myself, I knew all the answers. The hard part was accepting them.

The next morning when I woke up, reality had really set in. I was left to fend for myself yet again and again, nobody seemed to care. I began to spend more time at my older friend "Kelly's" house during the day so I wouldn't run the risk of the neighbors calling DYFS. The family was nice to me and I was fortunate because whenever they ate, they made sure I ate too. Her grandmother never really asked me questions about why I started to come over her house so much. Looking back now, I think she may have understood since she was a foster parent herself. None of the kids she cared for including my friend were biologically related to her. She was a very good person and shared a lot of love with me. I really thought I'd found family and friends until the day our friendship would be destroyed forever.

One evening "Kelly" and I went walking like we'd always done. There was an older boy in the neighborhood who'd had a crush on me. He was about the same age as Mosse and I was really intimidated by him. I would try my best to keep distance between us. This particular night, he had followed us all around the neighborhood. I knew that the word had gotten out amongst the neighborhood kids that I was "living by myself" since our house had become the hangout spot once the adults left months earlier. I knew he had to have this information and it made me feel like he was going to try and "get" me like Mosse used to. It started to get late, and I was nervous when I got ready to go home. Instead of me just leaving the crowd, I asked one of the girls if I could use the bathroom at her house (to try and throw the boy off from attempting to follow me home). When she said yes, I just headed in the direction toward her house and of course, the crowd followed. When we all got into the porch area, this older kid charged in after us! I was so scared, I followed my first thought: charge back at the boy swinging my fists as fast as I could. After about the third landed punch, he fell backwards out of the porch against the door and cut his eye against a deadbolt lock. Everybody started screaming and yelling until he sprung up from the cement steps and punched me right between the eyes! My vision instantly blurred but I just began to swing my fists again. Then, out of nowhere, the porch got quiet and I felt a yank to my left arm. The girl's mother had pulled me into the house. I looked down at my T-shirt to find it covered in blood.

When the police came, they took a statement from me and went to look for the young man (who'd vanished off into the night). Before the cops could come back to the lady's door, I explained a little about my situation. She had sympathy for the idea that I didn't want to go to DYFS, so with a promise that I would spend the night at Kelly's and go to where my mother was in the morning, she let us out the backdoor. We got to Kelly's house around 2:00 AM. Nobody was up waiting to ask us questions so we just went to sleep. In the morning, Kelly's grandmother woke me up and asked me what happened to my face. I told her I had gotten into a fight and dashed to the bathroom mirror. I was horrified when I saw my swollen face and two black eyes. It was the first time I'd really felt like I'd lost a fight. More than that, I was embarrass because I wasn't even with the people who was supposed to love me and had to rely on strangers to take care of me. I felt pitiful. When I came out the bathroom, I asked Kelly if she could walk me to the corner so I could go home and get dressed. She said, "What's wrong with you, why you ain't looking at nobody? Everybody knows you got two black eyes!" Without ever responding, I look up from the floor and straight into her eyes. All eyes were on me when I smirked at her and headed for the door alone. I never went back to that house again.

When I got out the shower, I noticed there were rat droppings on the foot of my sister's bed. All the thoughts I had of swallowing my pride and trying to "stick it out" flew out the window. I dressed and packed only the clothes I would need for the rest of the summer. On my way to the store for breakfast, I found a fifty dollar bill! Things seemed to be looking up. I called a cab to take me to Aunt Hope's, but when I got back to the building, Mah Mah was out front. She saw my face and started to rant saying, "What the hell happened to your face? Who did this?" After I calmly told my grandmother what happened and that I was okay, she took me home with her for about a week. She dropped me off with money and clean clothes to Aunt Hope's new apartment the following weekend.

At my godmother's new apartment there were only two bedrooms. My mom and Hank were there with Aunt Hope and Yasir's dad (my new godfather), so all the kids had to sleep in the living room, either on the couch or on the floor. It was me, Jihaad, Mumin, YaYa, and occasionally three more of my little cousins, whenever their parents wanted to get high all night. It didn't take long for the new apartment to became a full out crack house. All the kids stayed gone during the day doing everything from selling drugs and stealing bikes to make a hustle of bagging groceries and selling candy for the neighborhood retired drug dealers. After all my money was gone from the weed I bought off Mumin, I spent more time at the apartment, which meant I was breathing in more of the fumes from the drugs the adults used. Now my mother always had a hustle, so when she noticed I was low on cash, she took me out like she use to do when I was smaller. Only this time, she cut a deal with me. She asked me if I wanted to take a walk (and of course I knew what she meant). When she finally came out of the bathroom, we walked out toward the avenue to hit the bars. On our way she says to me, 'Sheenah, we gonna do it a little different today. I'mma get the money, all you gotta do is smile and be pretty and when we come back, I will split the money with you." By now, my mother and I had developed more of a "girlfriends" relationship so I responded back, "Yeah right. I might get ten or twenty after you rip me off again." She laughed and said, "Yeah, I used to rip you off, but you're older now and you need money. Pay attention, daughter. I'mma show you how to get a lot for very little." I was confused so I asked what she meant. She stopped suddenly and grabbed me by the arm with force. She said, "What the fuck is wrong with you, Sheenah?! You are a beautiful girl! Don't you know you have the advantage? A man would do anything for a pretty face. You just be sure YOU control all the doing!" And just like that, she grasped my hand and continued with me up the street. The rest of that day was a fog until we approached the pretty white van with the handsome caramel skinned older man in it. When he saw us approaching, his smile widened like heaven's gates. "Beauty, Beauty, Beauty! Look at this gorgeous thang walking toward me!" the man said to my mother. Momma smiled girlishly at the man and asked him what he was doing out in the neighborhood. "Looking for you." the man replied. "I been watching for the sunshine all day and here she is." Mom never really seemed moved when men complimented her so she responded, "Yeah I hear ya talking but I got things to do so I'm about to glide." Turning on her light pink kitten heels, she started back down the street and the man called her back saying, "Wait Mona, what's the rush?" My mother gave this man a story so slick about needing to get food for the house that he just gave her $100, two fifty dollar bills. Just when she thought she was going to move on to her next victim, he grabbed her hand and said, "Now let me take y'all to the store." That was music to Momma's ears, so we got into the man's van with him. We went from the grocery store to the shopping center to maybe two or three drug spots and then back to the neighborhood to the bar. We sat with this man for hours until my mother had gotten so drunk that she'd told him I was his daughter. Obviously, Momma had "history" with the man because he believed her. He started asking me all types of questions about myself and how I was doing in school. Before he finally let my mother free to leave the bar, he asked her if he could pick me up tomorrow and take me to meet my "sisters." My mother replied, "Yeah, if she wanna go." then motioned behind his back for me to say yes. I reluctantly said okay and the man gave my mother more money. We left the bar and went back to Aunt Hope's. Momma had over $300 but she only gave me thirty. They spent the rest of the night getting high while I and the rest of the kids slept.

The next morning, my mother woke me up to get ready for this man to pick me up. Terrified, I began to ask a lot of questions like, "Where is he taking me? Who is he? Why do I have to go, didn't you get your money?" My mother looked at me disgusted saying, "He ain't gon do nothing to yo ass! Just go with him and let him talk that shit! You know who the fuck yo father is! I'm tryin' to get you some money!" Before I could think, it just jumped outta me, "You the one getting all the money so why I gotta go?" My mother leaped all over me punching and slapping me. When Yasir's father pulled her off of me, Hank came out and asked what was going on. She looked at me as to say, "You better not say a word." Then she turned to him and said, "Nothing, she just getting too damn grown."

When the man came to get me, he was driving the same pretty van. He got out of the car as I walked up and he asked me if I felt comfortable. Thinking about the beating I just got, I told him yes but my real answer was no. Lucky for me, the man didn't have any ill intentions. He did most of the talking as we rode through city to city trying to find his daughters. Everywhere he seemed to look for them, they weren't there. This let me know that I wasn't the only girl with an absent father. After he introduced me to the girls, he bought me a pizza pie and sent me to the apartment with twenty dollars. Before I got out of the car, he told me he was glad he'd "found" me and hoped we could have a closer relationship. I did not reply so he asked me as I got out of the car if he could at least give me a hug. I said yes and he came around the passenger side and embraced me. The hug was warm and genuine and instantly, I felt sorrier for him than I did for myself. Momma suddenly appeared asking if we had a good time. When she walked up, I walked away feeling used and damaged. I felt used by my mother and damaged by the experience which was full of deceit and manipulation. The man obviously gave Momma more money because the apartment was full of addicts getting their fix. They beamed up from the early afternoon into the next morning. I never ate the cold pizza the man bought me.

When I woke up, I had an excruciating headache. As soon as I opened my eyes, the sense of light made my head throb. I could barely lift my head from the sofa, so I laid there for a few more hours hoping the pain would subside. When it didn't, I dug into my pocket for the money the man gave me so I could send Jihaad to the store for pain medicine and food. The money was gone. Jihaad had sympathy for me and bought me some medicine with his money from bagging groceries, but they didn't work. For the next two days, I struggled to raise my head and walk to the bathroom, let alone eat or attempt to leave the house. My mother noticed my pain and did nothing. The day after my headaches began, Jihaad complained of a rash. Momma hunted Uncle Mike down to get the Medicaid card and took him to the doctor. When they'd gotten back I asked why she didn't take me and she never even answered, just looked at me like I made her sick. I later found out that the man refused to give her anymore money and she'd blamed me for it. YaYa's dad felt so sorry for me that he'd given me one of his pain tablets to try and rid me of the headache. The next morning I was even worse, now vomiting and shaking with chills. I'd had enough! I laid across the couch, searching my brain for people I thought would possibly help me. Then that small voice whispered to me again and said, "Aunt Jacey lives around the corner."

Prayer
I'm out on my own and I know I'm alone,
I just need some help accepting it.
I'm out in the cold and my spirit's so low,
I just need some sunshine to settle it.
If it wasn't for life, I'd be much more serene,
But existence has got me belligerent.
I'm out on my own and reality's shown,
I just may as well get used to it!

CHAPTER 9

It took me more than an hour to get to Aunt Jacey's house. When I rung the bell, my cousin Bashir let me in. He was the youngest of Aunt Jacey's kids and the only boy. He and Jihaad were close in age and "hung out" together a lot in the neighborhood. Aunt Jacey was a no nonsense lady. She was still pretty and had grown mildly full figured over the years. Previously, she was known for a dashing smile, but she'd recently had all her teeth pulled. It didn't take away from her beauty though, so she would smile wide and speak loud possessing the same charm she had in her younger years. She and my Uncle Gipp split only a few years after their family moved out of the building. She could no longer take his abuse. Aunt Jacey never treated us different though. Through the years whenever we would see her, she would greet us with that wide smile and embrace us so tight it would cut off circulation. When I got up to the second floor apartment, Aunt Jacey met me at the door. "Baby, what happened!?" she asked, observing my head hanging over to the left side of my body. I burst into tears and my aunt led me down the hall to her bedroom. She laid me in her bed (dirty and all), fed me, gave me pain relievers and allowed me to rest in her bed until that evening. When I woke up, Aunt Jacey was sitting right beside me. She asked me what happened and out of nowhere, I began to share with her everything I'd been through living at Aunt Hope's new apartment. As she listened in shock and disgusted, she never offered me to stay at her house verbally. Instead, she left the bedroom for a moment only to return with clean sleepwear and tell me I could sleep in the girls' room for the night.

Aunt Jacey had six children, five girls and one boy. My youngest cousin, Bashir was the only boy. Then there were the five girls: Daaiyah, Faraah, Layla, Baainah (the child who broke her arm), and Nahlah. Daaiyah was the oldest and she had a baby at sixteen. She lived in the house with her mother and her baby was a little over a year old. Faraah was next to the eldest and she was very quiet and timid. She and I have birthdays a day apart. Laylah was the third eldest. She was born with a heart issue and always seemed to get along with everyone. Baainah followed Laylah and she was every outspoken. She was the only girl in the house I could remember who had friends outside of her sisters. Then there was Nahlah. She and I were a little less than a year apart and we were very close. We had a lot in common, from writing songs and poetry, to being the little sister, and experiencing a lot of "unfair treatment" from our older siblings.

After being at Aunt Jacey's for more than a week, nobody came to look for me. When I would call Mah Mah, I would discover that neither my uncles nor my mother even asked her about my whereabouts. This made me feel even more worthless and sad. I felt like my own mother didn't care about me. My uncles didn't really have to in my opinion (since no other male really did in the first place), but my own mother? Star was still living with Uncle Phillip and Tina and it seemed as though Jihaad was doing just fine without me at Aunt Hope's. I believe that was the first time I started thinking more about myself than about not having any other person. I started to wonder about how life would be if Aunt Jacey just took me in. I thought about how life would be if I went to school on a regular basis, studied hard, and eventually went to college. I imagined myself being successful and self sufficient, never having to be homeless again or rely on another person to secure my happiness. I even envisioned myself on a college campus, carrying books and going to classes, just like I sometimes do, staring out that window at Aunt Lattie's. I was only twelve years old but somehow I felt like I'd wasted a lot of time thinking about everybody else. This lasted for about a week. Then I was thrust out of that mindset when Star came knocking at the door.

Being at Aunt Jacey's was lots of fun. There was always lots of excitement and activities. Living there gave me a sense of myself being a female. My aunt had five daughters so I couldn't help but be conscious of things like wearing a bra, clipping my nails, and of course cooking and cleaning on a regular basis. Sure, I had exposure to all these realities in the other houses I lived in, but at Aunt Jacey's, it was A RULE to keep things clean. Her apartment was huge and there was always work to do. They blasted music almost constantly and that made housework easy for me. When we had downtime, we really had good laughs. It was as if every day, we were having "an orderly party," for lack of a better word. Lots of food, music, jokes and of course, chattering about being girls. I believe this is when I started to see femininity as a blessing.

Star ended up at Aunt Jacey's when Mah Mah spilled the beans to Uncle Phillip about me being with her. Tina couldn't wait to put her out again. I still believe she only let her stay because she wanted to keep the peace with Uncle Phillip. Star had always been his favorite niece even after he began to have children and Tina knew it. She also knew that in order to put Star out by herself (meaning without me or Jihaad), she had to make sure Star had a stable home to transition to. Me being already at Aunt Jacey's made perfect sense.

Aunt Jacey didn't have a problem with me and Star being there but when my mother dropped Jihaad off one afternoon to "play with Bashir," she took a different approach. My aunt pulled me into her bedroom alone and asked me, "Do you have anybody else you can call that might take care of y'all? I'm not kicking y'all out, but if somebody can help me, maybe somebody from your father's side, that would be good. I live here on public assistance and I don't have a lot. Do you have anybody's number?" I instantly thought about the time my mom gave me my paternal grandparents' phone number when I lived at Aunt Lattie's. I memorized it then, but I turned to my aunt and told her, "I know my dad's parents' name. Maybe we could look them up in the phone book."

Before we placed any calls to Olsten's out of the Yellow Pages, I told Aunt Jacey I never really had a relationship with anyone from my father's family. She still thought it was a good idea to give reaching out to them a shot. After calling nearly a half dozen S and M Olsten's, a lady picked up the phone and said hello. "Hello, is this the Olsten residence?" I said to the woman with a mildly Carribean or Southern accent. "Yes, it is," she replied. "Do you have a son named Sheppard?" I asked the woman. "Yes, I do," she responded. "Well, I'm his daughter, Hasheenah. I called you a few times a few years ago." "Yes," she responded, "how are you?" After I'd given her my reason for calling and expressing my desire to want to meet with her in person, she told me I could call back in a few hours and either she or her husband would talk to me then. When I got off the phone, Aunt Jacey gasped in surprise! "Why didn't you tell me you been talking to them? We could have called these people," she said. I then explained to her that I was ashamed that I had already reached out to them years prior and they never expressed a desire to want to see me. I felt myself feeling unaccepted again. My aunt consoled me, telling me that none of what had been happening or what had happened was my fault. She had a way of explaining life to me that made me feel like everyone around me was making a lot of mistakes and that I was so sad about it because they couldn't realize it. As odd as it sounds to me now, it made perfect sense when I was a kid. It empowered me and it helped me to not feel so sorry for myself. But those empowering feelings were often short lived.

When I called the number back, a man picked up the phone. I explained to the man who I was and the conversation I had with his wife hours prior. He was aware and seemed excited to meet both me and my brother. The man took down Aunt Jacey's address and about forty five minutes later, the doorbell rang. When I got to the door downstairs, I saw a brown skinned, stocky built, older gentleman with an aged face that looked very much like my father's. "Grandpa?" I said with a smile on my face. The man smiled back and opened his arms saying, "Nice to meet you Hasheenah."

Once I and Jihaad got acquainted with my grandfather, Aunt Jacey let us go with him to their house in the western suburbs. Shortly after our arrival, I met the lady with the distinctive voice over the phone. She was very beautiful and very well dressed. She didn't look like anyone's grandmother and she was eager to inform me and my brother not to call her grandma. She insisted that day that Jihaad and I call her "Nanna," and because of her stern delivery, we did.

We would spend lots of time with my grandparents after that. They took good care of us, taking us shopping for presentable clothing, giving us allowance and sharing lots of fun family history. They even took us with them to their family reunions and we gained a rich perspective of our family roots while learning about who my father really was in the process. That eased me in so many ways and the structure began to help me build confidence on a lot of levels. My grandparents were very strict, but it didn't seem to bother me because I never detected any malice in it. Sometimes, Jihaad wouldn't want to visit them saying, "they always trying to tell us what to do and how to eat and how to be." I agreed with my brother but I just figured it was because they were trying to teach us. Looking back, I felt that we were kids who lacked a lot of guidance. The guidance we did get was sporadic and made a great impact from people like Mah Mah and aunts Yolanda, Lattie, and Jacey, but we needed more consistency. Once my grandparents reconnected with my mother, who was now coming around to see us again, they decided they would help her secure housing if she regained custody of all three of her children.

Hank had gone to jail around the time my momma brought Jihaad to Aunt Jacey's and she'd start hanging out with this old man named Blue. Old man Blue had to be in his late sixties and he drove an old town car. Looking back now, I know he was Momma's "Sugar Daddy" or old guy who liked her enough to pay her for her attention. He walked with a cane and wore these thick framed glasses that seemed to lean to the side on his face. We were always afraid to go inside the house where he lived with his younger sister because they had a cat the size of a teenaged dog. I never really was too fond of cats and this cat in particular gave me the creeps. He was a friendly cat but I was so afraid of him, I always felt he would attack me. Old man Blue used to give my mother money, and of course she would get high with it. He also served as her personal taxi, taking her and her close family members all about town. He was nice to us too. He kept candy with him and always tried to be extra nice to us, trying to win a little more of Momma's affection. Momma used to tell us, "Don't get used to being around him 'cause when Hank gets out, he will be history. He's just a friend of mine and that's it." Old man Blue was very helpful in my mother getting custody of us. He would run her back and forth to court and to the legal offices for our documents. Once my momma got custody of us, I don't remember seeing him around much after that. My last real memory of old man Blue was him giving me a twenty dollar bill on my birthday. I just turned thirteen.

I remember the day I got the news that we would be moving into an apartment with my mother. I woke up for school, and just before me and Nalah left out, my mother was coming up the back steps. She was bright eyed and bushy tailed, dancing toward Aunt Jacey singing, "It's Been a Long Time Coming" by Sam Cooke. It was the first time I heard her sing since I left Aunt Hope's. She was boasting to Aunt Jacey about how our apartment would be done next month. I was ecstatic! It was like a dream come true! Finally, me and my family could really be together and be happy. Momma was in a ninety-day program for her addiction and all of her children were together, going to school regularly. God had truly answered my prayers! I was so happy that day, I went to school and told Ray, the boy who'd been pursuing me to be his girlfriend, that I would take him up on his offer.

Things were going great. My momma was consistent in her program, my grades were improving and I had a boyfriend with a goatie who was only fourteen years old. Ray was the first boy I would sneak off and be alone with. We'd go to the park and walk holding hands. He was nice to me and very handsome, but I was a little nervous around him because he looked older than he was. I would often joke about him lying about his age and he would always keep me laughing with his boisterous jokes. One night, while he was walking me to the gate near Aunt Jacey's, he asked me for a kiss. I began to shake and took a long time to answer. Bashfully, I looked down for a second and when I looked back up, he was in my face, nose to nose. Before I knew it, our lips touched, and he smoothly slipped his tongue in my mouth. I got a funny feeling between my legs, so I pulled away and took off running toward Aunt Jacey's. That was my very first kiss.

As soon as I got in the house, all the kids were telling me Momma had been walking around the neighborhood looking for me. I darted straight to the bathroom to pee and check my underwear. I looked down into my underwear and screamed! "Oh my God!" I belted out. All the kids rushed to the doorway to see me standing there shouting, "It's something in my panties!" My cousin Baainah walked over and looked in saying, "It's your period, stupid," then walked out. I stood there embarrassed and shocked. "How could this happen? All I did was get a kiss. My momma gone think I was a fresh tail girl and she gonna kill me." After Aunt Jacey and Star helped me clean myself up and get situated, they teased me and welcomed me to womanhood. I'd gotten my period.

About three weeks later, Momma came to Aunt Jacey's to move us into the new apartment. It was in the same town we lived with my uncles in and all we had were a bunch of garbage bags filled with clothes, some disposable plates and cutlery and each other. We moved in on a Sunday, and for the first week, we slept on a few of the bags we'd moved in with. It was only me, my mother, my brother, and my sister, finally. The next week, Hank had gotten out of jail and he came to move in with us. He bought beds for me and my siblings while he and my mother slept on the floor a few more weeks. Then one evening, Hank came home with a bed for him and Momma to sleep in. My grandparents had gotten some gently used furniture from my grandmother's youngest sister and before long, our new home was beautifully furnished and filled with lots of love. Momma enrolled us in school and Hank still worked his odd jobs during the day. Life seemed to be sweet until the day I came home from school to find my mother locked in the bathroom again.

CHAPTER 10

After the holidays, Momma and Hank stopped even trying to camouflage their drug use. I never saw Hank actually use, but he would nod all over the house, in the living room, kitchen, he'd even zone out in the bathroom and someone would have to bang on the door to snap him out of it. By now, Star is nearing sixteen, Jihaad is in sixth grade, and I was end the eight. A full-fledged tomboy. I wore my hair in either a ponytail and bang, or french braids, baggy jeans, and over-sized t-shirts, sweaters, and jackets. I spent most of my time reconnecting with my peers from grade school and still getting into fights, along with spending some weekends with either my grandparents or Aunt Yolanda. Aunt Hope died the summer before and Mumin moved across town to the northern part of the city with his girlfriend. Whenever he wanted to get away from her, he'd come stay at our house, sometimes for months at a time. Due to my previous fascination with hustling, it didn't take me long to start hanging around with some of the younger drug dealers in my new neighborhood (all of which were male). Being in that atmosphere gave me a deeper curiosity with weapons. While I wasn't hustling yet, I'd started to hold guns for a few of the dealers on the block and soon became known as "Taz" to the weight pushers for my reputation for "wilding out." Star and I didn't get along at all during this time. We were never really defined as being close but now, we would have several fist fights and countless clashings over our extreme differences. She'd become somewhat of a recluse in my opinion. When she went out, we rarely knew where she was or who she was with and she had no respect for my mother as a result of her addiction, so Momma was clueless about her acquaintances as well. Star would often fight Momma back whenever she tried to correct her behavior. She didn't say much to me, Hank, or Momma, unless it was in a belittling or offensive manner, but she was nice to Jihaad. My brother hang around some neighborhood kids and dealers too, but I don't think he was dealing at this time either. Neither of us really mingled in the same circles of friends but, Jihaad and I both knew each other's "crews."

One rainy day in March, I was walking home from the corner store and I noticed this boy following me. He followed me all the way home and just before

I opened the door to go inside he called out, "Sheenah!" Puzzled, I peered back at the stranger from a distance, confused. The closer the tall, brown kid jogged, I began to get familiar with his features. As he approached the cement steps, I smiled and so did he. He stood there, catching his breath and I asked both surprised and pleased, "Hey Selah! How'd you know it was me?" We spent the rest of the day on my porch just watching the rain and talking. Selah lived right down the street with his mother and two little sisters. I learned that day that he didn't call his mother "mom." Instead, he called her by her first name, Jackie. When I asked him why, he explained that she'd had him at fifteen, and because she was so young, his grandmother took care of him while his mom went to school. So as a baby, he began just calling his grandmother, mommy. This made me want to share more about my life with him. He didn't judge me or see me as a victim and it wouldn't be long before he and I would be inseparable. Shortly after I met back up with Selah, I would meet a person that would shift my life in a very peculiar way. Her name was Dinah. Dinah moved into the apartment above us with her two small children. She was barely nineteen and was moving in upstairs to get away from her abusive boyfriend. I remember us watching her and her sister moving things into the apartment from a compact car. They had to make maybe three or four trips but I watched as this small-framed biracial girl lugged bags and boxes up the flight of stairs with her seven-month-old daughter on her hip. After a few trips, my mother opened the front door to ask if she needed help. "No, I'm good, but thanks for asking," was her only response. Intrusively, my mother stretched her arms toward the child and said, "Come on, baby." Grabbing the two-year-old boy who had been following her by the hand, she smiled at Dinah and said, "Don't worry, they will be safe sitting here with us. We'll even leave the door open so you can see them." After Dinah was settled in, I would find reasons to knock on her door and ask her questions. At first, it was things like, "do you know if the mail ran?" and "did somebody ring your bell looking for us?" It didn't take Dinah long to see that I was simply curious about her, so one day, she invited me in. I played with the kids and she talked to me about school and what I wanted to do with my life. Without me even telling her, she knew things about what was going on in our house. She would encourage me by saying things like, "Right now, somebody else is in control. Later on, you will have control of your life. Work now to make sure you never have to deal with the pain you have now later on in life. I learned so much from Dinah. When she would let me babysit for her on occasions, she would teach me how to cook, how to scrub the corners of the floors, and even how not to be taken advantage of in relationships. She was very outspoken, but I admired her for her strong will and her ability to always make life look easy even when she was tearing at the seams.

When things weren't haywire at our house, I would spend a lot of time singing and writing music, sometimes with Jihaad. Over the years, we'd both grown a great interest in rap music. He would write his rhymes and recite them to me, and I would try and come up with choruses to go with the songs. Then I would secretly write rhymes of my own, but never found the bravery to showcase them until one day at a block party. I was nearing fourteen-years-old. I admit that a lot of the poems me and Nahlah wrote at Aunt Jacey's house were secretly raps, I'd simply slowed down while reciting, but nobody really knew that but me. But this day was different. I felt this overwhelming confidence that day in the cypher of rappers. Maybe it was because I really didn't hear any raps that intimidated me. Whatever it was, it made me move into the circle and nod my head with the rest of the guys. Again, I was the only girl but I felt right at home. When the teenager next to me was ending his rhyme, he included in the closing that he was gonna pass it to the "home girl next to him." Without hesitation, I started reciting a rap I'd written at Aunt Jacey's almost a year prior called, "MC Murderer." The whole crowd was yelling when I finished, and that built me the confidence of a lion! I was always writing after that.

That night, leaving the block party, I'd caught up with Jihaad and a few of his friends. The funny thing was, both I and my brother had started making friendships with kids who were older than us, which was a strange coincidence. Anyway, Jihaad and two of his friends kept attempting to walk a little distance behind me and I wondered why. After blocks of slowing down to let them catch up, I finally got frustrated enough to ask, "Okay what's the deal? What are y'all tryna hide?" The oldest kid pulled his arm from behind his back and asked me, "You wanna hit this too, Sheenah?" Without really thinking, I gazed at the marijuana cigarette and back at the boys. When I looked back at the brown wrapped cigarette, my hand went up. Putting the blunt to my lips, I took a short puff, held it short and blew it out. It was just like smoking cigarettes at Aunt Lattie's at first, and then I started feeling different. Not bad different, but strange different. Different like I was in a fog, and everything around me was calm, and simple things became every funny. We sat out on a slab of concrete in a vacant lot and finished the weed cigarette. We soon got hungry and headed to the corner store to get snacks. That's when I started to feel embarrassed. I didn't want to go into the store because I didn't want anyone to know I was high. I felt guilty for being older than my brother and setting a bad example for him. Then I started to think, "What if this wasn't his first time?" That thought calmed a lot of my guilt, so I felt like I had to act like I'd done this all the time too. We got the snacks, clowned around a little more, and then it was time to go inside. My mouth got dry and I started to feel scared. "She's gonna know I'm high." I thought to myself. "How am I gonna get past her? What if she smells it in my clothes?" While me and my mother had grown a very comfortable relationship, I still respected her and knew she would beat my ass if she felt I was out of line. When me and Jihaad reached the steps, he turned to me and said calmly, "Let me go in first, just walk right behind me and go in your room and don't say nothing." I nodded and followed his instructions to the letter. Plopping down on my bed, I realized my thoughts about Jihaad getting high before were true and miraculously, we'd gotten it all past my mother. The next day, I asked to hang out on Selah's porch. My mother looked at me in disgust and said, "Yeah you can go, but you bring your ass back in this house before the sun goes down. And don't make me come looking for you, you little bitch 'cause you will be embarrassed!" Feeling completely stripped off my dignity and ashamed, I said okay and darted down the street to tell Selah everything.

By the time school started, I had been smoking weed every weekend. Not with Jihaad, but with other teens in the neighborhood. Selah never wanted to be around me when I smoked. He always said smoking weed made me "different," and he didn't like what it did to me. He'd started to hang around with the local car thieves, and it was then that I started to branch out and find other associates. I soon started hanging out with a girl named Bella. She was one grade under me and she was a pretty brown skinned girl with big bright eyes. Most people thought she was quiet, but underneath she was funny, daring, and just as dangerous as I'd become. Jihaad hated Bella. He would call her names and try and keep her from coming to our house to see me. It didn't stop her at all, we were together a lot early on. She introduced me to drinking alcohol that summer. Then there was Kara. Kara was a hippy, pretty dark brown girl in my eighth grade class. She was outspoken, feisty, and always seemed to have a lot of friends. She also had a boyfriend who was older than us. She always tried to keep me out of trouble, but she always seemed to get into fights in school and in the neighborhood. Oddly enough, Kara and I never got into so much as an argument. This might have been because we were so much alike and had so much respect for each other. Bella and Kara were nice to each other, but they weren't friends. However, they would become my best female friends throughout high school. Ciara was my friend too. She and I had become friends during my freshman year. She already had a best friend but we would always hand out to do dirt. We smoked weed, helped the stick up kids do "drops" and get paid for it. I was the cool chick that made the guys comfortable. She was the sexy, bow legged girl the guys couldn't wait to get their hands on. She was the first girl that ever coached me on how to flirt with boys. We did it all the time when we set up drops, but she was more advanced than I. Nevertheless, our connection was serious and it never took us long to reel them in. We were lucky to never have to hurt anyone. Selah would become my best male friend, aside from being my occasional boyfriend—whenever he could handle my outlandish temper outbursts. When he couldn't, we'd simply go back to the friend zone. Then there was Jade. Me and Jade were two tomboys who "got into shit" together. She was a very pretty faced thick brown girl, but she was rough. She had a knack for crime and hanging out with her made it easy for me to just be myself. Oddly, her company always seemed to make me some money as well as get me into trouble. When I wasn't with one of them, I'd hang out with Dinah or my grandfather. I really believe that being around my grandfather a lot made my dad come around more. The funny thing was, my parents really started to get along and it didn't seem to bother Hank. When daddy would come to our house, Momma would cook for him, they'd play cards and even get high together. I learned my father was into drugs only weeks before we moved back with my mother. I happened to "catch him" coming from a drug spot on my way from school after his dad had summoned him to try and spend more time with his kids. From the first day I met my grandparents, they'd become permanent fixtures in both I and Jihaad's lives. My dad just didn't seem too interested on his own. Then one day, I just came home from school to hear Momma and daddy arguing in the house. Jihaad came in shortly after and Momma just kept yelling, "No, tell them the fucking truth, Shep! Don't lie to your kids, they need to know! Tell them today, Shep! How long we gon talk about this shit? It's been two years!" My dad looked over at the door where me and Jihaad were standing and then he stood up from the table and walked toward us. As he opened the door, he looked down and whispered, "I gotta go, I'll be back." He jumped in his car and sped away as my mother kept screaming, "He need to tell y'all, I'm tired of this!" About thirty minutes later, my dad pulled back in front of the house blowing the horn as he always did. I pulled my body up from the couch and it felt heavy. I looked out the window to see my father standing outside the driver side of his car while it was still running. I knew it was bad news. The lump in my throat grew, my hearing seemed shallow, and my hands were clammy. "This is gonna be bad news, I know it." I thought to myself. I walked out the door with Jihaad following behind me. Then, I pretended to fix the bottom of my oversized jeans so I could savor the time of "not knowing." When I finally stood in front of my father, his words were, "Your daddy got something to tell y'all. Your daddy got the virus." Jihaad said okay, and I just stared at the ground. I felt like God had played a very cruel game with my life. As soon as my daddy had a chance to come into my life and actually protect me and be there for me, I had to hear that he's gonna die and he may never get the chance to show his love to me like I'd always longed for. Daddy jumped in his car and sped off. Jihaad walked up the street and I stood there in the street, angry. When I finally got the nerve to enter the house, my mother met me with all the dialogue I didn't want to here. "See, I told y'all something was wrong. Your daddy is dying." and all kinds of cold and inconsiderate things. Before I knew it, I belted out to my mother, "Okay, shut up, Mah! Damn!" and slammed my bedroom door. She busted in after me ranting, cursing, and angry. I felt as if she was angry about the idea that I cared or maybe that I didn't have an emotional response like crying. At this point in my life, I viewed crying as a sign of weakness and defeat, and if it was anything I didn't want to be, it was to be weak and be defeated. She went on some more, and as I tried to tune her out, she slapped me! I looked up at my mother, shocked and confused, and before I had a chance to react or even cover my face in protection, she started to pound on me like I was a stranger. She was punching and kicking me so fast, all I could do was tuck my body in a ball as I fell from the bed. Hank rushed into the room and pulled her off me. He had to pick her up and carry her out of my room that day. I just laid in the floor and sobbed. I felt hurt, embarrassed, ashamed, confused, and a host of other emotions I can't really even describe. My mother never apologized to me for that day. In fact, we never spoke about it again.

My Prayer

> *God, what's going on? Why does it always seem like as soon as something goes good for me, two things go wrong for me? I know they say don't question God, but how else will I know if I don't ask? Am I doing something wrong? Why would You bring my dad back into my life if You knew You weren't going to let me enjoy him? I know things could be worse, but I feel wronged by You. Can't you work something out that daddy won't have to die? God, Please! Do something!*

By now, Momma and Hank's drug use was full throttle and frequent. To add to that, Momma started to drink beer every day. Mah had taken sick around this time and spent several months in and out of the hospital. We found out he had ovarian cancer only a few weeks before she died. Her death made me very numb. I didn't know whether to resent her, or grieve her so I spent a lot of time avoiding the loss all together. I would tell myself her husband's car broke down and that's why she hasn't been by to visit, or she's broke and don't have any money to give us so she's staying away. That made coping easier, temporarily. After Mah Mah died, Momma would drink every day in addiction to getting high, and when she drank, she'd become violent and extremely talkative. For some reason, I always seemed to be the one she picked to take her anger out on. There would be times that she would get high and then get drunk and come outside looking for me. When she would find me, she would torment me all the way home only to get there and pick a conflict with me about not listening to her or thinking I was tough. Then she would beat up on me. I never thought about fighting my mother back like my sister did. I loved her too much and I didn't want to hurt her, but I did wonder why she never was as combative with Star and she was with me. I must admit, a lot of the times I didn't want to hear what she was talking about because she spent a lot of time talking about the past—people who'd hurt and used her, people she'd trusted that let her down or betrayed her and often times, those people where her family members. I didn't want to necessarily hear my mother's stories but I didn't want to disrespect her so I listened to the lessons; lessons of not labeling everyone a "friend" and not being too trusting. Sometimes her conversations would keep me up until the wee hours of the morning. When she would get tired of talking, she'd make me sing with her. I didn't like that either because she was always making me sing her favorite songs over and over again. It was rituals like these that would blossom me and my mother's relationship into somewhat of a "girlfriends/ confidante/ enabler."

Not long after the episode with my mother, my dad stopped coming around as much and when he would, it would really be only to get high with my mother. I would spend a lot of time with my grandparents on the weekends and I even worked for them during the summer months, but during the weekdays, I hang out with the drug dealers. One afternoon, I traveled across town with my boy, "Bunch." Bunch sold drugs, weed, and dope. I had no idea we were going to "pick up" until I entered the house through the back entrance. A tall guy opened the door and he and Bunch shook hands. He looked at me and said, "what's going on, Shortie?" and I followed Bunch down a dim lit hallway. I entered the living room and saw a coffee table full of white powder and an open duffle back of ziplocked packages of marijuana. The man sitting at the table looked high. He looked out the top of his dark shades and said to Bunch, "What up, Fam!" The man stood and they embraced. Bunch said, "Sheenah, this is my cousin, Clark." I shook his hand too and sat at the table like I knew him. They both looked at me and started laughing as if they were both amused and surprised at my response. After they talked, we all sat at that table and smoked a lot of weed that night. Then, Bunch grabbed his purchase and we left. When I got home, it was shortly after 11:00 PM. When I walked in the house, Momma started wailing on me! I was so high, the licks didn't even faze me. I just let her go off and when she finished, I went to my room, kicked off my boots and fell out sleeping with all my clothes on. The next day, I spent a lot of time thinking about the night before. I thought about how good I felt "just being one of the fellas." I made a decision that day that would alter everything. I was going to cop my own drugs.

CHAPTER 11

I had been selling weed during and after school for a couple of months now, plus I decided I wanted to work at my grandfather's office for three hours a day after school. I finally had my own money so I decided to get a bank account. At fifteen years old, I was depositing my own money into that account every week. Some of the money came from selling the drugs but most of it came from working with my grandparents. I was small time so the drug money was my play money. This was just money to spend at the bar or on new clothes. I started getting my hair done professionally now too. I had a beautician for each of my hair dos. I wore my hair wrapped, flat twisted and in a French roll. I was really feeling independent and secure until the day my mother walked into the kitchen and announced to the three of us she was pregnant.

It was the early-mid nineties and I'd really started liking boys. I had a few boyfriends after my eight grade first kiss, but none of them were serious enough for me to be curious about sex yet. Selah and I were boyfriend and girlfriend but due to the fact that we were both "in the streets," we were more like buddies who kissed each other. He'd started stealing cars the years before and spent a lot of time in and out of juvenile hall. I started to get bored with having a boyfriend that was always absent, so I looked around at other options. I had a crush on a boy two years older than me from the neighborhood but he told Bella that I acted too much like a boy, so I had to forget about him. Ciara would try her best to "soften me up" over the years but it never seemed to work. She'd try to buy me lip gloss. Take me with her to stores for fancy girlish clothes and such, but I was never interested. I didn't want to look too soft because soft to me meant defenseless and vulnerable. I wanted to be strong and in control and this went against my theory of strength. Then there was a boy my age named Jean. Jean was tall, dark, and handsome. Every girl in the neighborhood and in school liked him. Somehow, he chose me, but only for a second. We dated for a few months, and when I didn't want to have sex with him, he dumped me. Soon after my mom found out about the break up, she started to label me gay. One afternoon, she and my dad sat down with me to have a meeting about my sexuality. Daddy didn't say much, but

I could tell by the tone of the conversation that we were only having it because my mother thought they should confront me. Daddy asked me, "Do you like girls or boys, baby?" I answered that I liked boys and my mother cut me off, ranting again. "You don't gotta lie to us! We gonna love you regardless! I'm your mother, I know you!" On and on she went until I made up in my mind that my new goal would be to find someone to take my virginity. Maybe then, she'd stop making me feel so uncomfortable.

A lot of boys liked me because I was "cute" or "cool" but the truth was, I didn't like any of the boys who liked me, except Jean. I was very particular when it came to dating and boys. He had to be quiet, kind of tough but not mean, respectful, and of course cute. Not many boys in my school or neighborhood fit this bill, but Jean came really close. So one night, after a house party, I got Jade to tell Jean to come to Dinah's apartment.

When Jean came to Dinah's house that night, I took him to a room and asked him to break my virginity. He asked me if I was sure and if I was sure, do I want it to be him. I answered yes to both and then he asked me why. I looked him in the face and laughed and said, "Trust me, you wouldn't understand." The next day, I pondered on how I was going to tell my mother. Leaving my bedroom that afternoon, I felt the timing was perfect. She was sitting in front of the television in the living room, cutting potatoes, and I plopped down next to her very casually. As soon as she looked at me, I blurted out, "I had sex with a boy, I'm not gay." She gasped for air and dropped both potato and knife. Tears filled her eyes and she sprung up from the sofa. Letting out a long sigh, she said, "What?" As my heart sank, I said it again. My mother stood there, tears rolling down her face and shaking her head. "Damn! I'm being judged again." I thought. She picked up her knife and potato bowl and walked into the kitchen whispering, "Okay." I got up and walked out. Before I could even get off the porch, I was smoking a blunt. Walking down the block that day, I began to question my own sexuality. I searched my thoughts to see if I'd ever found a girl attractive even once. I pondered on my thoughts concerning women, even myself and thought, "Maybe I am gay and just don't know it." I took myself on a mental and emotional journey that day back down through years and situations, decisions and outcomes, and concluded, "I'm too high to be thinking about this shit right now! Fuck that, I'm about to get high."

My dad's health took a turn for the worse right after I lost my virginity and I started to blame myself, thinking maybe he knew I'd "done it." I thought maybe it had broken his heart so I told myself I would never have sex again. I didn't get much enjoyment out of it when it did happen so why would I need to now? I was selling drugs less now because after school, I worked at the office and after that, grandpa would take me to see my dad in the hospital. I have three girls from the block who looked up to me selling my drugs so I had a little change coming in from that. Most of what they made, I paid out back to them and just kept the flip money. I think I did it that way out of guilt of doing to some other little girl what Holly and Tye did to me without even knowing it. I would see my dad just about every day and now he couldn't talk. There's a condition with HIV/AIDS that develops over time when the tongue become coated with a thick white substance and this condition had gotten so bad with my dad that it made it hard for him to talk. For months, I would go and see him and do all of the talking. When I wasn't talking, I try and play music or just sit with him. He always looked to be angry or uncomfortable but whenever I would hold his hand, he'd look over at me and smile. Early on, he'd even wink his eye and that would mean a lot to me. One day after leaving the office with grandpa, I visited my dad in the hospital and upon my arrival, I walked up to the bed, smiled, kissed his for head. His eyes looked so happy to see me; it was like this day, he recognized exactly who I was! He grabbed my hand and his eyes shined! I looked down at my father feeling like royalty. Finally, he was happy to see me instead of the other way around. He held my hand, occasionally squeezing and rubbing it. After some time, grandpa left the room to let me be alone with him. "This is my chance." I thought. Without hesitation, I started to tell my father how happy I was to see that he knew who I was today. I told him how happy he made me when I'd walked through the doors and how much I loved him just for being my daddy. When I started to cry, I started to talk to my father with my eyes. I felt like through the windows of my eyes, he could feel my soul. Maybe he knows that I loved him so much that I'd reserved that love for him and no one else. How being his only daughter was the only time in my life I'd ever felt favored by God. How that was the only thing I ever felt was just for me. Tears streamed down my daddy's cheeks and I felt the strangest pull in my stomach that let me know instantly our bond was forming but our time was extremely short. Grandpa entered the room again and I hadn't even noticed until he whispered to me, "Sheenah, it's time to go." I leaned over and kissed my father on his cheeks, forehead, chin, and lips. All his wrongs toward me were gone instantly. Then, I attempted to break my hand from his grasp and he wouldn't let my hand go. It took about twenty extra minutes and a nurse to get my father to loosen his grasp and his eyes never left mine. When grandpa dropped me off at home that night, I got extremely high of marijuana all alone, but nothing could numb my feelings of despair.

Because I had been MIA from the block for a while, I was oblivious to the rumors of Bunch getting high on bigger drugs. It wasn't until one day, walking out the corner store, an elder in the neighborhood pulled me to the side and said, "Baby, I know you think you got friends, but these people you around ain't nothing but trouble. Watch the company you keep." I ignored her and continued up the street behind Bunch. Later that night, we went clubbing and got high and drunk.

A few days later, Bunch and I were hanging out in the hallway of the building he hustled out of. We started talking about drugs and I was explaining to him the effects of different drugs. By now I was more aware of the different type of "highs"; been exposed to drugs all my life and now selling them. I guess I thought I was competent. That day, Bunch told me he was curious about taking a "stick." After he gave me more knowledge, I agreed to try it with him. I'd grown so daring and fearless as it related to drugs in general. The next evening, we met at the local chicken shack and headed back to the building. He split the pill in half and gave me a piece. I opened a can of beer and drank it down with the drug. Before I put the can to my mouth he said, "put it under your tongue first." I did exactly as he said as I drank the beer and could feel the tingling both on and above my tongue. Then I swallowed the pill down. I sat down on the step next to Bunch and we just laughed and joked about really taking the drug. Minutes later, he got up from the step and went outside to make some sales. Soon, he called out my name for me to come out front. When I got up from the step, I felt extremely light. I felt like everything was a dream, but a really good one! When I got to the porch all I could see was fog and it took me a minute to focus. I started to hear my name being called almost like I was in a movie. Bunch was down on the corner, at a red car waving for me to come on. As I trotted down the stairs, I felt like a horse. A strong one! I was gliding and celestial. It felt like everyone and everything was pleased with me. I don't even remember if I was smiling, but I felt happier than I've ever felt in my life! I was so calm and easy. As I got into the car, I remember seeing white plush leather everywhere! I sat down and in my mind, I reclined myself. Now we were riding. As the car moved, I felt myself drifting up and down like a very smooth roller coaster. All my movements were smooth. My voice was smooth. Even my breathing was smooth. The driver turned the music up and I felt like a star! We rode for a little while and then Bunch had the driver to drop me off at home. When the car door opened, I felt this rushing feeling and I felt completely disoriented. The next thing I remember, Bunch had rang my doorbell and took off running back to the car. I realized it was my house when my mother opened the door screaming at the moving red car, "What the fuck did y'all do to my baby!"

My mother managed to get me into the house and on the sofa. I was completely out of it. I still felt the "coast" but with every movement, my body couldn't catch up with my mind. I tried to tell my mother I was sorry. She hushed me and told me to keep my voice down. Then she asked me some questions, "Where were you? Who were you with? What did you take?" She then pulled off my boots and yanked my shirt up. She carefully examined my body. Then she put her hands down my jeans and ask me did anybody get my pants off. All I could do was shake my head no because while I couldn't really speak fast enough, I remembered everything that happened. I don't remember if I answered all her questions but whatever I told her made her lay me across the sofa and watch me sleep a few hours. The next day, I woke up feeling very hungry and I had a headache. It had to be close to 2:00 PM before I got off the sofa. When I did, my mother fed me and ran me a bath. We didn't talk much about my drug use that day. All she kept saying was, "Don't do this shit, Sheenah. You don't wanna do what I do with your life." About a month later, Momma gave birth to a baby girl named Fareedah and Hank went into rehab. His son, Latif, moved in with us as soon as he came home.

A few months later, my father died. At his funeral, I was a complete mess. I spent a lot of time crying that week. Then it really started to dawn on me that he was gone for real. I remember being so angry, I planned to go outside and provoke someone to fight me. After a few hours, a guy I didn't really get along with satisfied my rage. The fight resulted in me cutting him with a broken bottle. He needed several stitches to the left side of his head. I was seventeen. My anger would ignite even greater when Momma married Hank two months after my dad died. I was the only one of my mother's children not in the wedding. While I loved Hank for being good to us, my grief wouldn't allow me to celebrate. Hank seemed to understand, my mother on the other hand wasn't. I would go on to get high even more now. My senior year, I was up to smoking at least five blunts a day and taking at least two pills. Now I was taking hits (codeine) because the high lasted longer. I still went to the prom but I found out I was not going to graduate on time. The fight I had would bid me a very serious aggravated assault charge. At my trial that spring, the judge read her verdict. She pulled up in her chair and gazed at me a moment. She then said, "I don't know why I'm doing this young lady but God must truly be on your side. I'm not going to send you to jail today, but if I ever see you in this courthouse again, I will see to it that you do five years in the women's correctional facility." My mother and I stood holding hands and shaking and as soon as she finished talking, I promised the judge that my days of menacing behavior were over.

When school ended, I took up full time employment at grandpa's office. When I wasn't doing that, I was hanging out and getting high. My interest in drug dealing had seriously dwindled because my attention was on getting high so I stopped having the girls hustle for me. The money I would use to pay them and flip went on my pills. I was now up to about eight pills a day. When I wasn't high, I was in some bar or in some fight. I finished up my high school credits at the local night school. When I went back to my high school to get my diploma, I ran into one of my old teachers. I remember having a crush on him but I made sure he never knew it. Over time, the crush dwindled due to my preoccupation with drugs and running the streets. A year or so later, I'd taken a few of his classes again and he'd become very nice to me. Before the end of the school year, I had to take his morning class for graduation credits. It was then that we'd formed a positive student/ pupil relationship. He even met my mother at a banquet at the school. When he saw me at the school picking up my diploma, he congratulated me on sticking to my goal and finishing school. Then he told me he wanted to take me to shoot pool as a way to celebrate. My mother had met him prior so I told her about him wanting to take me to shoot pool. She said it was okay with her and I already checked with him to see if Bella could come too. He seemed to be okay with that. On the day we were supposed to go with him to the pool hall, Bella backed out at the last minute. I didn't want to seem rude so I went anyway. When I got into his truck, everything seemed normal. He asked me about my plans for the future and what my goals where. Then, he told me he had to stop at his house to get something. I told him I would wait in the car but he suggested I come in. When I got in the door, I felt instantly uncomfortable. I stood at the door while he moved about the house as if he was looking for something. Then he comes out with a stack of papers. "Can you please type these warning notices for me?" he asked. Reluctantly, I said yes and he led me through a kitchen to a typewriter. I sat down and began to type as fast as I could. The whole time I was typing, he was talking to me. He had even turned on the television to a basketball game. I had secretly made up in my mind that as soon as I was finished typing, I would make up an excuse to leave and get back home on my own. When I was finished, walked to the threshold of the living area where he was sitting and held the papers up, telling him I'd finished. Now, he was sitting in the dark and asking me to come and sit next to him. My heart tensed up and my hands got clammy. "Oh, no!" I thought. "I gotta get the fuck outta here!" Before I could turn and head for the door, he'd grabbed me by the forearm and spun my body back toward him. I felt terrified. Here I was in this house, with this big muscular man who's a good fifteen to twenty years older than me and I felt helpless. The closer he tried to pull me, the sicker I got. As I turned and yanked away from him I said, "What are you doing?" He replied, "You know I want you." Then he grabbed me around my waist and with one hand, pulled my shirt over my head. I could tell he'd done that to someone else before so I started to beg him to let me go. My pleading had no effect on him. It seemed like he'd gotten more aggressive. He was so big, I didn't want to make him feel like he needed to beat me or kill me so I just cried silently. After he'd pushed me on the couch and pulled off my jeans and underwear, he mushed my panties in my face and told me to stop crying. I held my breath and warm tears rolled down the sides of my face into my ears as he entered my body. I felt five all over again. I laid there hating myself for not fighting him. So I had to think of some defense. Every time he whispered sexual things in my ear, I spoke back into his saying, "No. Stop. You are wrong, I don't want you to do this." That was the only defense I could come up with. When he finished raping me, he got up from the bed and went into the bathroom. Moments later, he came out with a damp washcloth and told me, "Wipe yourself off with this. Then get dressed so I can take you back where I got you from."

When I got out of the car, I went into my house and took a hot shower. I had to be in there for an hour trying to wash him off of me. After I dressed, I walked straight back outside unnoticed. As I walked down the street rolling my marijuana cigarette, the first place stop was to the pill spot to cop a dose. I got extra high that night, but no matter how many pills I dumped or how many blunts I smoked,

I couldn't escape the images in my head. They played over and over in my head, him snatching off my shirt, him pushing me to the sofa, even him raping me. Occasionally, my crew I was getting high with would ask, "Sheenah, what's up? Where you at tonight?" I would shrug it off and make jokes about them sweating me or being "all in my grill." I walked home that night around 2:00 AM. As I turned the corner to head on my street, I started thinking of ways to kill myself. My life was already over. So much had already happened to me. I was already scarred. I was an eighteen-year-old drug addict who'd been abused in every way imaginable and now raped. And what was worse was, nobody knew it but me. I was always too afraid to speak up for myself when it counted. Sure, I could wild out and fight but that only seemed to punish me, time and time again. I thought about the many times people hurt me, tricked me, disappointed me, embarrassed me, and even lied to me. I got mad at myself for being a victim all over again. "What's the point?" I thought. If I died tonight, nobody would even miss me. By the time I got to the front door, I had a plan in place. I went to the closet and got the gun Ali left in my closet before he went to prison last summer.

The house was quiet, with the exception of the music coming from my mom's bedroom. My little sister, Fareedah, was still a baby and Momma was pregnant again. Now, nobody paid attention to any of the older kids in the house. I walked right back out the front door with Ali's gun. Sitting on the stoop of the vacant three-family house, I stared off into space, thinking of all the reasons I should die. I thought about how in my life, it always seemed as if the only love I'd ever gotten was either forced or tainted. Momma didn't love me more than drugs, but I loved her more than life. Daddy didn't have time for me but he was all I ever thought about. I was always set apart from my siblings and the only time I've even felt a bond with them was when something was going wrong in our lives. Mah Mah did the best she could but even she got tired of me and the only reason my grandparents even acknowledged me was because I pursued them for a relationship. In my heart, I'd had enough! Then my stomach started speaking to me. It said things like, "That was never you're fault. You are set apart because you're special, you have a gift. You're stronger than you think you are. God gave you an innate ability to survive and He did it because He's not tired of you. Stay in the game, things will get better, just wait and see." With every negative thought came a positive affirmation in my spirit. Then I pulled the gun from my waist and laid it in my lap. My hands started shaking and my mouth got dry. I was afraid now because I knew I was going to do it. I shut my eyes and picked up the gun. Pointing the gun to my stomach, I felt a warm sensation fall over me. Then I leaned over on the gun and pulled the trigger. "Click!" the gun sounded as I exhaled all the breath from my lungs. I laid there still with my eyes shut and holding my breath. Then I leaned up and looked down at my shirt. It was clean. Then I opened the gun to find that it was never loaded. "HA, HA, HA!" I burst into laughter! "Why you ain't check that before you left the house, Sheenah?" I thought as I laughed hysterically for at least <u>twenty minutes</u>. Then it was time to get high again. I lit another blunt and smoked it to the neck before I went in to bed.

My Prayer

> *God, I think I now know what they mean when they say "God is merciful." I think sometimes, shit just happens for a reason and when it does, we gotta learn how to just live through it. I almost really ended my life with my thoughts and now I know that I can also begin my life again with them. I just don't know if I am brave enough. You keep telling me I'm strong, but after looking over how much shit I let "ride," I don't really think I'm brave. Sure, I take chances and I can shut down enough to get angry and set if off, but anybody can do that if you give them a bad enough grief or a big enough audience. Plus, I get high and it really starting to show now. The sad part is, with every passing day, I'm starting not to give a fuck! What can people do to me that ain't already been done? I don't care no more. Just long as I don't die and go to a lake of fire, I'm good. I hope you understand . . .*

A few months later, Aunt Yolanda died. She'd gotten sick with cancer only a month prior to her death. Ali was still in prison and didn't get to make it to her funeral. The last visit she and I made to see him was a week after they diagnosed her. She made us vow to live our lives like sister and brother in the event something happened to her. At that time, we laughed at her and made jokes saying, "Chill, ain't nothing gonna happen." I guess you could say she warned us. Ali and I had always been close so of course I continued to visit and send money when I wasn't running the streets. I started to use so much now that I was barely working with my grandparents and I was always penny pinching. I went from being the one bringing the drugs to being the one scouting for them. Then, one day my grandfather pulled me in his office on a rare occasion I did work and asked me to go on a college tour with his church. "Grandpa, I don't have no money to pay for that right now." I said to him gazing around the room. "If you commit to actually going, I will pay for everything." was his response. I agreed to our deal and left to go home for the day. When I got high that night, I clowned with my friends and had a good time but I couldn't help but think about me and grandpa's deal. For the next week, I was scarce at the office. Grandpa called me that Sunday night and said, "So, I guess you're not going, huh." "No, I'm going," I replied. He said, "If you were going, you would be there right now. The bus leaves from the church in an hour." I asked him if he'd already paid for me to go and he said yes. Before we ended the call, I told my grandfather I would be on the bus before it pulled off. I hung up, packed my bag for a week and darted down the block to get some drugs to hold me for the trip. When I got to the bus stop, the bus was just pulling off. I hailed a cab and had the cabbie drop me off a block and a half from the church and I jumped out without paying because I run out of money. When I got to the church, all the youth from the college ministry were on the bus and my grandfather was standing in the lobby in a pair of sweats. He'd just gotten there to pay my balance and he wanted to be sure I was going to show up. As I was sprinting toward the church, I saw my grandfather's smile widen through the glass doors. I ran into the church and wrapped my arms around my grandfather and whispered in his ear, "Told you I wouldn't break the deal." We came out of the hug and he stuffed two hundred dollar bills into my hands as his eyes filled with tears. When I boarded that bus, my life changed. Yes, I got high the entire trip, whenever I could get off to myself but little did I know, my whole story was going to soon make sense. My mom had given birth to yet another little girl named, Fatima, this same year and I thought about the example I would be setting for both my little sisters if things went well on the trip. My mind went to so many possibilities and I'm glad they did because occasionally, sitting under some teaching taught me that as a man/woman thinks, so he is and whatever you think will be. I ended up singing for one of the choir representatives at a small HBCU in South Carolina. He and the director liked my voice so much they offered me a vocal music scholarship. They assured me that if I raised my GPA in my first semester to a 2.5, I would get the full allocated amount per semester. In fall 1997, I began my studies in Child and Family Development in September 1997. I stopped getting high on pills and marijuana and graduated with a Bachelor of Science degree in 2001. Then I went on to graduate school and attained a double Master of Arts degree in Human Resources Management and Human Resources Development. At both graduations, I remember thinking about how I dreamed of doing this when I was a child. I thought of all the times people, including myself told me I couldn't do it. I remembered all the pain I endured, how many gave up on me and how many God had taken away. I felt grateful because I had the opportunity to see God move in one of the most dismal and unpromising situations that was my life. I was humbled because I knew that God had a plan for me even when I wasn't doing and acting in a way that was pleasing to Him, that He was going to have me realize His plan for my life. I felt so powerful and powerless at the same time understanding that, God had given me strength through my pain and God Himself is truly alive in every situation! This is when God was effervescent . . .